MW01614780

The Well-Trained Heart

Ray and Donna Reish

Training for Triumph Publications

The Well-Trained Heart
published by Training for Triumph Publishing

Cover by BP Digital Creations
Printed in the United States of America.

For more information about curriculum items (including character-based language arts and composition books), parent teaching tapes, and additional materials written by the Reishes, contact:

Ray and Donna Reish

Training for Triumph
6456 E US 224 Craigville, IN 46731
(260) 597-7415 trainingfortriumph@mchsi.com

www.tfths.com

Contents

Section III: Well-Trained Heart How To's

Section IV: Homeschooling With the Well-Trained Heart Approach

Introduction

This fall (2007) marks the twenty-third year of homeschooling for our family--even though our oldest child just turned twenty-five. We began homeschooling in 1983 by teaching my younger sister in our home during her eighth grade year. Through the years we have watched the trends in homeschooling--beginning with homeschooling in the early eighties because of the desire to keep our children with us instead of sending them away--and the desire to control what they were taught. To a longing to provide proper and sheltered socialization opportunities. To the trend in developing a love for learning and school. To the idea of academics not being important; character was all that mattered. To the years of competing with Christian schools, trying to prove that homeschooling was as academically sound as "going to school." To the more recent movement of an unbalanced focus on academics. We have watched it all and even joined some of the bandwagons. Yet through it all, we have consistently returned to the method of homeschooling that most of us began with in those early years: focusing on the whole child with an emphasis on teaching our children to put God and others above self--training the heart well.

This method of homeschooling, first taught (possibly without even realizing it at the time) by such godly teachers as Raymond Moore and Gregg Harris, has served our family and countless others through the myriad trends, years, and trials of homeschooling. We have chosen to call it "the well-trained heart" approach, not to de-emphasize academic training--but rather to put the heart training front and center--where we believe God places it. Join us as we teach homeschooling parents what we believe are the most important aspects of homeschooling: those that affect the heart--and as we help to put the other aspects of homeschooling in their proper perspectives.

Front Notes

1. This book is a joint effort of both homeschooling mother and father; however, constantly saying who is saying something (i.e. Donna or Ray) and constantly changing voice and verb tenses becomes laborious for the reader to follow. Donna will be doing the primary writing (speaking for both of us) though technically it is Ray who qualifies us to write this book at all. Unless it says otherwise, *I* refers to Donna; *we* refers to Ray and Donna. *I* and *we* will be used alternately.
2. As a language arts curriculum author who has taught thousands of children to write in the past eight years through our language arts and writing programs (*Wisdom Booklet Language Arts*, *Character Quality Language Arts, and Meaningful Composition*) and a copy editor who edits over ten thousand pages of text each year, I am extremely aware of grammar and usage errors. One of my most bothersome pet peeves is incorrect subject-object agreement. More and more writers and publishers are succumbing to the easier-to-read and comprehend method of disregarding the he/she battle when using singular subjects and later objects (i.e. *A student* should enjoy school and do *their* work thoroughly rather than A *student* should enjoy school and do *his or her* work thoroughly). I am, however, unable to bring myself to do that! So...a student or child will be a *he* throughout this book (unless I am referring to one of our daughters or information that applies to female children only), and the homeschooling teacher (in spite of the fact that Ray teaches many of our school subjects, especially Bible and discipleship) will be *she*.
3. If you recognize ideas, tips, and advice from others, they

probably did come from others. We are not psychologists, Bible scholars, or family counselors. We give credit where credit is due; we would not have developed this approach to life on our own. Thank-you goes to those who have gone before us in the homeschooling and Christian parenting world and taught us literally everything we know: Terry and Esa Everroad, Dr. and Mrs. Raymond Moore, Bill Gothard, Gregg Harris, Ron and Rebekah Coriell, Jonathan Lindvall, SM Davis, Ken Ham, Dr. Tim Kimmel, Gary and Ann Marie Ezzo, Kevin Leman, Reb Bradley, Norm Wakefield, Ruth Beechick, and many, many more.

4. From the list of experts above, you can see that we have learned from a wide variety of sources. One of our "hobbies" during our first dozen or so years of homeschooling was going to conferences and listening to teaching tapes (as well as reading books) about homeschooling and parenting. We have, through the years, listened to and read advice from dozens of people, and we quote or refer to many of them in this text. This does not mean that we adhere to all of their teachings. It has been our experience that the homeschoolers who are the most successful are those who can listen to or read from a variety of homeschooling and parenting experts and take just what is needed for their families and leave the rest. No judging, no "all or nothing" type of listening and reading--just assume that each person is wrong in some areas, but God can use what He desires for us, and we can leave the rest. We ask that you do the same with our book.
5. Kayla and I teach research paper writing and are putting the finishing touches on a research paper book, so I am extremely familiar with the MLA style of documentation. It is necessary for research based writing, but it is not always the friendliest writing and notation style. Because of this, you will find a mixture of MLA formatting and "Donna formatting" within these pages. Again, it is our desire to make *The Well Trained Heart* as user-friendly

and helpful as possible that drives us to a certain style or format. Thus, some aspects of the WTH may not seem exactly MLA-styled, such as these informal front notes and the combination end notes/verse references in the back of the book. (The latter was done so you would have all verses in their entirety together in one place in the order they appear in the text.)

6. At the end of each chapter, you will find discussion/application questions. These may be used however you deem most helpful to you. We would love to hear that small groups of homeschooling parents all over are reading and learning from the WTH--and meeting to discuss the chapters and make applications to their families with accountability and diligence. Regardless, these questions are there to help you ponder what each chapter contained and to aid you in making personal decisions for your family.
7. Our style of writing might be different than what you are used to reading. When I was a young homeschooler and I read homeschooling books or went to conferences, I wanted details--what works, what doesn't, specific examples of the author's methods, etc.--and you'll notice that those are the things we refer to when we describe something we learned from early homeschooling experts. That is why we write like we do. We want to give concrete help and advice. We want to give examples of what has worked and what has not. We want you to have actual help you can take with you, not just theories or abstracts.
8. In keeping with our user-friendly approach to writing, we have included dozens of little tidbits and examples from our own family and homeschooling experiences. In these instances, we often name one or more of our children. It became laborious to include incidental information within the text about their ages, birth order, ministries, education, and so forth. Thus, those details are listed below (in "Our Family"), at the time of the writing of the final draft (January 2008).
9. Lastly, a word about the title. We began taking notes for

this book several years ago, some thoughts here, some examples and ideas there. It had a working title of *The Relational Homeschooler*, which I never thought adequately described this heart training approach. Around that same time, I read Susan Wise Bauer's helpful book, *The Well-Trained Mind* (WTM). After reading the WTM, I thought to myself that the homeschooling community needs information about not only training the mind well but also training the heart well--then realized that our approach to homeschooling is just that, the well-trained heart. So, in titling this book *The Well-Trained Heart*, I in no way wish to diminish the WTM's message but rather desire to supplement it. Let's help homeschoolers in training the mind well *and* training the heart well. And if these two should ever be incompatible, let's focus on the heart.

Our Family

Ray--married to Donna for twenty-six years; homeschooling father for all of his children's lives; originally trained in accounting (CPA and CMA); the model of well-trained heart fathering

Donna--married to Ray for twenty-six years; homeschooling curricula author for eight years; originally trained in elementary education and reading education; constantly learning to be a well-trained heart mother

Joshua--currently twenty-five; married to long-time homeschooler Lisa (Prentice) for three years; first born "guinea pig"; earned bachelor's of arts in history in 2005 through testing out of all but two classes; residential and commercial painter, cottage class teacher, writer, speaker, and editor/ typesetter.

Lisa--first daughter-in-law; currently twenty-four; married to Joshua for three years; homeschooled all of her school days; artist, part-time worker for us, teaches art classes in our cottage classes

Kayla--currently twenty-one; second child, first daughter, second "guinea pig"; homeschool language arts curricula author for seven years; soon to graduate from college with RN degree and biblical studies degree; teaches sciences, writing, apologetics, and Spanish in our cottage classes; in teaching ministry and Spanish ministry at our church; speaks for us

Cami--currently twenty; third child, second daughter, third "guinea pig"; working on degree in church ministry with an emphasis in disability ministry; on staff at our church as disability ministry director (One Heart Disability Ministry); teaches sign language, piano, guitar, speech, and writing in our cottage classes; speaks for us as well as for the disabled; volunteer as family retreat leader and area planner for Joni and Friends ministry

Kara--currently seventeen, finishing her last two years of high school; fourth child, third daughter; participates in various drama ministries at home and throughout the US, as well as disability ministry; teaches speech and writing in our cottage classes; speaks, writes, edits, and typesets for us

Jonathan--currently fifteen, freshman in high school; fifth child, second boy; participates in drama ministries and disability ministry; customer service worker/order filler for us; learning to speak and write for us

Josiah--currently twelve, in sixth grade; sixth child, third boy; participates in drama ministries and disability ministry; does secretarial work for us

Jacob--currently nine, in third grade; seventh and final child, fourth boy; makes us all laugh and smile; keeps Mom and Dad young

Dedicated to our seven children--Joshua, Kayla, Cami, Kara, Jonathan, Josiah, and Jacob--who have given us their hearts to train well

With deepest gratitude to Raymond Moore and Gregg Harris, who introduced us to this incredible lifestyle

ONE

Don't Go Breakin' My Heart

What Is the Well-Trained Heart?

DEFINING THE WELL-TRAINED HEART

What Is It?

Defining a child with a well-trained heart is like trying to define what a Christian life should look like--because a homeschooled student with a well-trained heart should have a life that looks, well, "Christian." But even that is vague, especially in our society today where over eighty-five percent of people surveyed say they are Christians.[1]

The well-trained heart is one that has been held, protected, and nurtured by the parents--until the child is ready to protect and nurture it for himself. It is one that was given voluntarily to wiser, stronger, and more capable people (his parents) until the day it grows strong enough to face those things that young hearts should not have to face alone. And then, in due time, it is a heart that is given back to the young adult when he is wise enough, strong enough, and capable enough to go it alone.

A well-trained heart resides within the son or daughter who is taught from an early age to love that which is good--obedience, kindness, deference, thoughtfulness, empathy, and other godly character traits. It lives within the child who is trained to live his life for God and for others--regardless of what his future occupation, social standing, family situation, and education level may be. It lives within the student who sees his school years as preparation for a life that glorifies God--not himself. It lives within the boy or girl who is constantly reminded (and develops the belief within himself) that "it's not all about him." Thus, he gives himself fully to God and others. It lives within the young person who studies, trains, and learns because he enjoys being diligent and reaching goals--since he knows those studies and early training opportunities will lead him to a life that will be worth living.

Moreover, the well-trained heart is one that has been prepared academically, morally, spiritually, and socially to become all that God has planned for that person. It is not a heart that has neglected academic training or socialization. However, in a well-trained heart, academic and social skills have been developed in a way that God and others remain in the forefront of the child's life--and in a way that helps that young heart grow into an adult heart that spends its life serving rather than being served.

It Begins With You

Of course, all godly training begins with the Lord. But once God begins His work in us, preparing us to train our children's hearts, the heart training of our children begins with us. It is up to us parents to begin, little by little, giving to our children what the Lord has poured, and continues to pour, into our hearts. This is, of course, the most difficult part--and the reason that so few parents train their children in this way.

Homeschooling already requires a level of parental example that no other method of education requires. Quite frankly, our children see exactly what we are--and measure daily how close what we are comes to what we say we are. Because of this, it is challenging to live with our children in the way homeschooling provides--and still place character and lifestyle expectations on them. We know our children know us, I mean truly know us, and we often feel inadequate to expect a way of living from them that we ourselves may not be able to (or are not willing to) attain.
But in the truly well-trained heart home, this transparency does not end the training--it actually begins it. You see, a heart-training parent cannot have religion and rules only and pass them on to his or her children. It simply will not work. (Oh, it might work for a while with younger kids, and might even look like it is working with older ones, but many times these rule-dominated children are "standing up on the inside" even when we are making them "sit down on the outside.") A heart-training teacher knows her failures and shortcomings--and still exposes her heart to her children anyway. These unveilings are springboards for the training of her children. Those failures and inadequacies become ways of saying, "Look, I am human too. I have trouble living a life for Christ also. But let's try to do this together."

Heart-training parents do not impose a set of rules and religious checklists onto their child in the hopes of gaining that child's heart. You see, it is getting into the heart of the child that makes a parent successful, not regulating the outside.

Reb Bradley, veteran homeschooling father, speaker, and author, addresses this topic in his essay entitled "Solving the Crisis in Homeschooling":

> It is also possible that they see the shallowness of our "religion" and are not attracted to it in the least. Christianity is not a system of do's and don't's - it is following a wonderful Savior who gave his life for his people. A legalistic faith consisting primarily of "avoid this, wear that, and attend this" is not attractive to most children. Such children grow up full of knowledge and rules, but lack attraction for the Lord Jesus. They may identify themselves with Christ at an early age, but it is possible that the Christianity they learned from us was characterized chiefly by religious rules and doctrines. They will eventually forsake their identification with Christ because they grew up under the weight of religious standards, but lacked the grace and power to carry them out. Many such young people have forsaken "religion," and still need to find Jesus and the grace of salvation.[2]

A DIFFERENT WAY OF THINKING AND PARENTING

It Requires a New Way of Thinking

If you truly want to become a heart training homeschooler, the place to begin (after submitting yourself and your life completely to God's service) is within your mind. We could all train our children much better if we were able to rewind, erase, or at least store elsewhere for a time all of our preconceived ideas about education, child training, success, and even life. Unfortunately, that isn't likely to happen, so we have to force ourselves to look at things differently.

Thought Processes

There are several thought processes that are incompatible with training our children's hearts well. One of these is thoughtlessly adopting man-made methods as our own. We have to remember that so many of the things we do and the ways we do things are technically man-made. Like the mantra that has been preached to teens forever, we homeschooling parents need to learn: "just because everyone else is doing it, doesn't make it right."

For example, why do children go to school at age five? (Now in some cases at age four, and in some states for the entire day, five days a week.) Is this based on solid research? Is this determined by some scriptural authority? Is this a result of long-term studies showing that going to school all day at age five builds strong minds, strong bodies, or strong social skills?

Or, how about driving? In our state, students may get a driver's license at age sixteen. Other states allow students to drive with an adult at age fourteen! Is it truly safer to have children drive at fourteen than it is at thirteen? What about eighteen? Is it safer for people to only share the roads with young people who are eighteen or older?

School age, driving age, voting age, dating age--these are all man-made. Yet, most of us assume they are right without question. Many man-made "rules" (written or unwritten) need to be followed as good citizens--we cannot allow our children to drive before the age adopted by our state; we must school our children 180 days a year in many locations; we are supposed to provide "equivalent instruction" to the public school beginning at age seven in various areas. It is showing good character and citizenship to obey laws that do not contradict God's laws.

However, embracing such ideas without measuring them against God's Word (which reveals God's way of living) is not good parenting. It is unwise--and will often *not* result in children with well-trained hearts.

Throughout this book, we will expose you to many ways of thinking that Christian parents have adopted unthinkingly, from having child-controlled homes, to pursuing education for the sake of education, to measuring success by the world's standards, to the best ways to develop true and meaningful socialization in our children. If we desire to raise children with well-trained hearts, we must look at accepted, man-made ideas and goals differently---and be ready to adopt different ways of thinking if they will lead us closer to our homeschooling and parenting goals.

It Is the Approach of Royalty

In recent years, movies and books focusing on princes and princesses have become widely popular. Many of these point to a way of living for royalty that is, well, royal. They often reveal a higher calling in the life of those given such rank. The children and young people in many of these books and movies are taught in specific, concentrated, untypical ways compared to those around them. Training is more purposeful; expectations are far greater.

How much more important should the training of God's sons and daughters be? We are called a "royal priesthood"[3] in Scripture. We are training our children to be royalty! We should not shy away from the difficult path, the higher road, the responsibility-laden life. We should teach and love our sons and daughters as though they will be serving in the court of the highest royal King--because they will be.

Oftentimes, we forget this concept. We think that our children should have it easy--that we should make them happy and comfortable as opposed to raising them to meet the difficult challenges of serving in God's royal court. I think it is interesting to note that those in royalty do not apologize for the demands on their children. They make it clear from the beginning that their family is "different"--and they will be held to higher standards, have to meet unusual challenges, and represent the royal family in style. We should train our children to be the princes and princesses they are called to be.

It Requires a Biblical Approach to Parenting

A strange thing happens when we parent our children in a non-biblical way. They become spoiled. But it doesn't stop there. Spoiled babies and toddlers become bratty preschoolers. Bratty preschoolers become surly elementary children. Surly elementary children become selfish teenagers. And selfish teenagers become self-absorbed adults. It simply continues throughout our lives---and we live lives that are unfruitful and self-gratifying rather than fruitful and others-oriented.

To avoid this domino effect, it is imperative that we learn and practice a biblical approach to parenting that results in children with well-trained hearts. Throughout this book, we will elaborate on this biblical parenting and life-long discipleship of our children because it is the foundation to heart "holding" and proper heart-training. Gaining our children's hearts in such a way that they allow us to "enter" and influence them to live godly, "one another" types of lives requires a truly Christian approach to *parenting*.

Many books and teachers instruct parents in how to parent effectively and, often, what they view as scripturally. But if the end result of that parenting is not selfless, character-filled living, are those approaches truly "Christian" (Christ-following) parenting? If they are harsh and unloving, could it possibly be God's way of parenting? There should be major differences in our parenting approaches compared to the secular world. But in true heart-training, there will be even another level of parenting exceeding nominal Christian living---that which focuses on the heart and on teaching children to yield their lives to God.

Below are some key differences between worldly or non-biblical parenting and parenting for the well-trained heart. We call the first one child-centered or indulgent parenting. The latter we will simply call WTH (Well-Trained Heart) parenting. Note that the WTH approach is more than the typical "putting out fires"-"keeping our children out of trouble"-"raising successful kids" type of parenting.

Indulgent Parenting	WTH Parenting
Focuses on me	Focuses on Christ and others
Teaches self-indulgence	Teaches selflessness
Teaches immediate gratification	Teaches longsuffering
Focuses on frivolities	Focuses on things of eternal value
Desires to make children happy & comfortable	Desires to help children learn to deny themselves
Raises children in a materialistic lifestyle	Raises children in a selfless, giving lifestyle

Indulgent Parenting	WTH Parenting
Teaches that others are lower than we are	Teaches that others should always be first
Teaches self-sufficiency	Teaches that without God, each of us is nothing
Attempts to make child happy	Helps child learn contentment in all things
Lives for the next thrill	Sees thrills and fun as rewards for hard work and service
Teaches minimalism in work and service	Taught to give all--maximum living, work, & service
Encourages children to declare personal rights & ownership	Encourages children to realize all belongs to God--teaches yielding of rights & ownership

It Is Most Effective When Begun Early

Many of the tips and pieces of advice in this book refer to starting when a child is young. Obviously, any new approach, whether it is homeschooling, new house rules, or changing a child's focus from himself to others, will be more difficult to implement in older children. But this is not to say that it cannot be done. We truly believe that older children's hearts can be turned to their parents and families--and to God and others--when Mom and Dad fully submit to God's new training in their lives, and the children (even teens) see that their parents are humbly submitting their lives to a new approach.

Yes, we are all born with sin natures. We all constantly do the things we do not want to do and do not do the things we know we should, as Paul reiterated in Romans 7:15: "I do not understand my own actions. For I do not do what I want, but I do the very thing I hate" (RSV).[4] However, we are all born with desires and capacities to know and love God as well.

So, for those of you with preschoolers and younger children, your work will not be as difficult as those with older children when it comes to heart training. But it will begin with biblical parenting (described above and other places throughout this book) and consistent discipline. Contrary to many parenting philosophies, we do not gain our children's hearts by being buddies with them from birth. This approach will not magically transform them into obedient children and, later, submissive teens who love, respect, and trust us enough to give us their hearts. Children are born helpless and foolish---which is why they are given to adults to raise. If we begin heart-training early, by expecting obedience and submission and giving loving, gentle discipline, then later heart-training and mentoring will be genuine possibilities in our homes.

THE WELL-TRAINED HEART APPROACH BEGINS WITH LOVE

If You Love Your Child, You Will Discipline Him

I remember early in my parenting, when I had one little girl who was, well, stubborn. She required so much punishment that I often grew weary of it--and frequently questioned what I was doing in her training. I can remember over and over again telling her that the Bible says in Proverbs 13: 24 that "He who spares his rod hates his son, But he who loves him disciplines him promptly" (NKJV).[5] In addition to being stubborn, she was also wise beyond her years (not sure why she wasn't wise enough to obey!). Anyway, she always agreed that, that was what the Bible says--and that if I didn't punish her I hated her. The bottom line is that if we love our children--and truly want the best for them--we *will* discipline them.

A Sacrificial, Character-Based, Unconditional Love

Of course, all parenting begins with love. But well-trained heart parenting begins with the biblical "love your child enough to punish him"--then moves into a type of love that few people in our world have ever felt or given--sacrificial, character-based, unconditional love. It is a love that says, *I understand that I was given you to nurture in order to bring glory to God, and I will do anything--and I mean anything--to carry that out.*

In the well-trained heart approach, the love is sacrificial because it requires more time, effort, and energy than any other parenting approach. Additionally, it is sacrificial because it requires us to put our own wants, hobbies, education, careers (even dads too, at times) and financial aspirations aside until our children are grown and no longer require so much of us (which is much longer than if they went to school at age five or we gave them up to allow other people and peers to influence their hearts).

This love is character-based. It is a love patterned after Christ's love rather than the world's--one that is characterized by behaviors similar to I Corinthians 13 (gentle, kind, selfless, humble, non-irritated, etc.) and the "one anothers" of Scripture. This love is not secured through belittling, yelling, arguing, demanding, etc. Certainly, non-homeschoolers can love their children according to these parameters too, but it is more difficult when the children are away so much and the parental influence is lessened simply by time constraints. Homeschooling offers us a precious, concentrated opportunity for more character-based love.

Finally, this love is unconditional because even though we have made our hopes and aspirations for our children clear--that they would live lives of selflessness and service--our children know that we will always love them regardless. They understand that, of course, we would be disappointed if they chose a more selfish path, but that it would not change our love for them. In the “rules and regulations” model of parenting and homeschooling, too often our children feel that we love them if they "make us proud" by following our external rules, but "crush us" if they do not or if they embarrass us in some way. This unconditional aspect of love may be the most challenging for homeschoolers because we often put too much emphasis on our children pleasing us.

In his book, *Grace-Based Parenting*, Dr. Tim Kimmel describes this depth of love for our children as *secure love*: "This is a steady and sure love that is written on the hard drive of children's souls. It's a complete love that they default to when their hearts are under attack. It's the kind of love that children can confidently carry with them into the future."[6]

The type of love required to train our children's hearts well can be obtained by all believers. Obviously, it is hard work, but it is also a supernatural work. If we desire this type of love and are willing to "do the hard things" to live and love in this way, God's Word says that we can pray for these changes to take place in us. This is clear many places in God's Word, such as in Romans 5:5: "Now hope does not disappoint, because the love of God has been poured out in our hearts by the Holy Spirit who was given to us" (NKJV).[7]

Not a Guarantee or Magic Formula

Back in my more authoritarian days of parenting, I often quoted "Train up a child in the way he should go; and when he is old, he will not depart from it" (Proverbs 22:6) (KJV)[8] to explain that if we were training our children "in the way they should go," they would not disappoint us; they would remain faithful to God and our teachings. After years of debate training with our children and after more thorough explanations of hermaneutics by Kayla, our resident Bible student, I have come to believe that this is not necessarily so.

First, let me assure you that I believe the Bible with all my heart. But, I no longer believe in picking random verses and making them promises to me straight from God or in making them doctrine (unless they were intended to be so).

If we pull Proverbs 22:6 out and make it a literal promise, then we would also have to literally believe other verses in Proverbs are promises. For example, when it says that we will be wealthy if we honor God, we will be wealthy. Well, we have tried to honor God in our lives, and we are far from wealthy! Does this make God a liar? Does this make his Word untrue? Of course not.

The laws of hermaneutics demand that when we attach a certain meaning to a verse, we find other Scriptures to back that one up, other verses that say the same thing. There are other verses on parenting that seem to indicate that proper training in children *will* yield favorable results, but there are also others that suggest this is not always the case (i.e. the prodigal son[9] and Adam and Eve,[10] which are pictures of God as a Father; surely he did not "mess up" in his parenting!).

I no longer believe that if we do everything "right," our children will always follow God and our teachings. I do believe, however, that Proverbs 22:6 shows us that the likelihood of having faithful kids is increased if we point them in the right direction when they are young. I also believe that if we approach our children in much the same way that God has approached us, we have a better chance of gaining their hearts--just as God has gained ours.

No, the well-trained heart approach is not a guarantee that our kids will serve God and others their entire lives. It is not a magic formula or ten steps to successful parenting. It is, rather, a way of thinking, living, and loving that we have found to be the most satisfying, biblically-sound way of homeschooling our children--with rewards far more vast than any other method we have seen--or could have ever imagined.

So...Don't Go Breakin' My Heart

In a nutshell, the well-trained heart is one that has been protected and trained. We have, within us as parents, the power to protect and train our children's hearts--the power to keep our children's hearts from being broken unnecessarily and the power to train our children's hearts well.

"Don't Go Breakin' My Heart"
Discussion/Application Questions

-- Chapter 1 --

1. In the past, have you valued spiritual training and heart training over all other types? If so, how have you done this? If not, how can you start doing so?
2. Do you try to hide your shortcomings or do you use these as springboards for training your children?
3. In what ways does your life show that following Christ is superior to other ways of living? How do you show your children relationship with Christ rather than religion?
4. What man-made benchmarks and ideals have you adopted? Do these benchmarks or ideals have a biblical basis? A logical reason? A research-based foundation?
5. Re-read the indulgent parenting vs WTH parenting list. Discuss how you might be contributing to your child's self-centeredness by focusing on his foolish desires, over indulging him, instilling in him a desire for his own way, etc.
6. What can you change in your life in order to have more time, money, and energy to develop the well-trained heart lifestyle in your family?
7. How much emphasis do you place on your children following your rules to keep you from being embarrassed vs. reaching into their hearts with unconditional love?
8. Do your children feel that you will love them even if they disappoint you?

TWO

Journey to the Center of the Heart

How We Discovered the Well-Trained Heart Approach
Part I of II

OUR BEGINNINGS

Our Life Together Began Young

Our journey to the center of the heart began long before we started homeschooling twenty-four years ago (in 1983). No, we were not homeschooled ourselves with the well-trained heart approach. We were not even raised in Christian homes. As a matter of fact, both of our families faced many trials and difficulties as we grew up. (Actually, through the years of learning the well-trained heart approach with our own children, we have also learned how to have develop close relationships with our extended families now as adults.)

Both of us grew up quickly. We had roles to play in our struggling families, and we both sought to fulfill those roles. Ray's same-age half-brother was the school athlete, and Ray became the school leader. Responsibility, diligence, and kindness were Ray's hallmarks even as an unsaved high schooler. I had three younger siblings to tend to while my mom worked two jobs.

But even more impacting on our future parenting was the fact that we have been together, well, forever. Ray and I were high school sweethearts. Falling in love when he was seventeen and I was fourteen, we quickly began planning our lives together. Four years later, shortly before our wedding, we found Christ--together. In many ways, it feels as though we have always been together and always served the Lord--together.

Honeymoon

Several months before we were married, we were born again in a quaint country church. We were immediately surrounded by Christians who loved us and cared about us. It was an amazing start to a life with Christ.

Shortly before we were married, our church hosted an evangelistic family. They came each evening for a week and taught about marriage and family living. We went to every session. We saw things in them that we had not seen before--especially in their children, whom we discovered, were homeschooled and traveled with them, sharing God's message for the family.

I still marvel at God's blessing on our young lives: we actually took marriage and parenting audio tapes from this family on our honeymoon with us and listened to them as we traveled. Before we ever had children, we were learning from a homeschooling family how to have a godly marriage and raise children in biblical ways.

Early Marriage

When we were first married, we were surrounded by caring, loving, godly people. A major key in our future life came out of this time: we were discipled by three couples (ten, twenty, and thirty years older than us) week in and week out--often daily. True discipleship like that permeates a person's life and makes a lasting impact on that life.

It is remarkable how the discipleship, love, and mentoring we received as young, married Christians have continued to influence our lives on so many levels for so many years. It provided the example for us of how to mentor and disciple our teens and young adults over the past few years. Through multiple times of hearing how important these people were in our lives, our children understand the impact that Christians can have on others through lifestyle discipleship. In celebration of our twenty-fifth wedding anniversary, we took all of the kids to visit these people in our hometown. Following that, two of our daughters independently of each other, wrote on their blogs how amazing it is to them that because of these people, their parents served God their whole lives and have now discipled their children to do the same. Each one said she was writing it with tears in her eyes as she realized that without these people in her parents' lives, she would not be where she is in the Lord (or in life) either.

EARLY PARENTING YEARS

Knowledge Over Character

When our first born son was young, we wanted everyone to think we were good parents. We wanted to show off how smart and clever our little guy was. So we religiously taught him God's Word.

Now, we were not having a lot of success on the obedience issue, but he was definitely smart, and we wanted everyone to know it. By the time he was four years old, he could name the kings of Judah and the kings of Israel, give Elijah's speech to the worshippers of Baal, and recite the Ten Commandments. It was so fun to show him off!

About that same time another family of traveling evangelists (Terry and Esa Everroad[1]), came to stay with us for a couple of weeks as they ministered in our area. They had an incredible marriage and awesome teens and preteens who obeyed them and loved them. We respected them and wanted what they had, so we asked them to tell us what we were doing wrong. We gave them permission to tell us our blind spots, correct us, and help us improve in our marriage and parenting.

The first thing they said startled us: They told us that while we were working hard to teach Joshua the Bible, we were not training him in obedience and character. They reminded us that he did not come when he was called, stay in his bed when we put him there, and eat what he was given. They also pointed out that we had a tendency to ask Joshua when we wanted him to do something rather than telling him and expecting him to do it.

This was humbling to us, as you can imagine, but it marked the beginning of us adopting a biblical approach to parenting. We realized that we had been focusing on knowledge rather than character. We were more concerned with measurable, praise-able results than we were with long-term, sometimes-subjective results.

Authoritarian Parenting

About that same time, many young families joined our church from another body. These couples had been instructed that a child should be taught to obey from an early age--and that children should be immersed in the Bible by their parents at home. The authoritarian parenting that they modeled for us early in our child-rearing days was actually helpful to us, even though it is not what we ourselves exclusively practice or teach today. We had no idea how to parent, so when we saw our peers spanking their children for disobedience, we followed suit.

More importantly than that, however, we saw these parents religiously teach their children the Bible. They had morning devotions and evening devotions. They kept their children with them in church, giving them opportunities from early ages to hear the Word of God. And we did the same.

Granted, our parenting lacked much of the heart training that we know today, but for young parents of a preschooler and baby, we were getting started on the basics---at least the basics of training young children. And this was a good place to start.

OUR FIRST HOMESCHOOLING EXPERIENCE

Jumping Into Homeschooling With All Four Feet!

After meeting the Everroads and some of the young families who started attending our church, we began investigating homeschooling. I was about to graduate from college with a degree in elementary education, and we already knew that I would not work for the time being. We wanted our children to have a mom home with them during their early years. Plus, as I was getting my degree, I had left Joshua every day for most of his first year and a half of life. We didn't want to repeat that with future children.

A week after I graduated from college, we went on a vacation, and one of the new families from church sent some of Dr. Raymond Moore's books with us. I pored over those our entire trip, sharing with Ray each evening what I was learning. I could not believe how consistent his teaching on how children learn, boys vs girls, class size, etc. was with what I had been learning over the past couple of years in teacher's college.

When we came home from that trip, we were convinced that homeschooling was the way to raise children for the Lord, protect them from negative influences, teach them God's Word without a teacher at school teaching something different, etc. We were immediate homeschool advocates!

How immediate, we had no idea. Shortly thereafter, my mom was having trouble with my eighth grade sister who is cognitively disabled. Lisa refused to go to school because the other students were making fun of her. My mom would leave for work in the morning, assuming that Lisa was going to school, only to find that she had not gone. She was at a loss as to what to do since she couldn't keep taking off from work to get Lisa to school or come home to discover that Lisa did not go to school at all that day.

Hewitt-Moore Curriculum--"Home Grown Kids"

So, we volunteered to homeschool Lisa. We were twenty-one and twenty-four years old with one toddler in tow, but we knew homeschooling was the answer! At that time, getting homeschooling curriculum was nearly impossible, but we signed up for the Hewitt-Moore program[2] through Dr. Raymond Moore,[3] the aforementioned man who is considered to be the "pioneer" of the modern homeschooling movement.

I would have to say that this was my first introduction to homeschooling in a more personal way. Yes, we believed homeschooling would help us protect our children from negative influences. We believed homeschooling would give us the opportunity to teach them God's Word more. We believed it would give us the chance to teach from Christian materials rather than secular ones. But I didn't see the relational aspect of homeschooling until I filled in the forms for Hewitt-Moore for Lisa and received our materials and course of study.

One of the first things that struck me about the application for curriculum was some of the unusual questions we were asked: *Is your child happy with whatever he is given to eat--just as happy with an apple as he is with a brownie? Does your child enjoy helping you around the house? Is your child cheerful towards those he meets?*

Then when we got Lisa's program, we found it to be a well-rounded mix of academics, Bible teaching, and relational living. It had a daily suggested schedule of Lisa and I reading together, Lisa reading Bible stories, Lisa helping me with household chores, the two of us doing projects and service together, and other "personal" homeschooling applications. It was so different than the academic-only program I had expected. (It should be noted that Lisa made more “academic” progress in math, reading, and language arts that year with this approach than she had in the previous three years of school combined, according to a yearly achievement test administered by Lisa’s elementary school principal, who tested Lisa as part of her doctoral dissertation.)

Of course, after reading other works by Dr. Moore, I discovered that his whole approach to homeschooling was relational. It was about parents and children learning, working, and growing together. It encompassed the whole child. It focused on each child's academic, spiritual, and social needs. It considered a child's interests and hobbies. It was relational homeschooling. It supported the well-trained heart.

Character Training at the Fore-Front: Ron and Rebekah Coriell

During our year of homeschooling Lisa, a church in our community sponsored a one day workshop featuring a homeschooling family. We went, hoping to learn more about homeschooling, but what we learned would stay with us forever: *character is the most important thing you can teach your children.*

This couple, Ron and Rebekah Coriell,[4] taught us how to teach the Bible to our children, how to instill character in them, how to have harmony in the home, and so much more. They were new to homeschooling, too, having recently pulled their children out of a Christian school. But they had already learned the most important principles of Christian homeschooling.

The thing that predominantly stood out to me (besides their darling little girls doing memory verse recitations that would melt your heart!) was something I have never forgotten. They recounted the story of how they told their young daughter that she should choose white milk at lunch every day but one. On that day, she could get chocolate milk instead of white. At lunchtime one day, their daughter mentioned to a classmate that she wished she could have chocolate milk, but she had already had it once that week. Her friend urged her to get a chocolate milk anyway---saying that her parents would never know about it. This young girl's response made me realize that this was how I wanted to train my children for the Lord: "No, they wouldn't know, but God would."

From our first year of homeschooling, in spite of our community having just a handful of homeschoolers (and by the beginning of that next year, those would be gone because of persecution and threats), we were immersed in a relational approach to homeschooling--one that placed godly training over everything else, one that focused on training young hearts well.

The Christian Homeschooling Workshop and the Institute in Basic Life Principles

After the year of homeschooling Lisa• (and spending an afternoon with Dr. Moore when he came to defend homeschoolers in our town who were being threatened with jail, child removal, and more), I understood much more about homeschooling than one would think a twenty-two year old young mother would in those early homeschooling days. Then, as a result of all of the badgering of homeschoolers in our city, homeschooling died out in our area. Everyone either moved, went to public school, or started Christian schools in their churches. I felt all alone.

At that time, I read Gregg Harris' book, *The Christian Homeschool.*[5] Then Ray and I went to Harris' basic and advanced workshops. Continued confirmation that homeschooling was more than academics and punishment! I remember vividly when Mr. Harris recited a sample schedule of his son Joshua's school day: math, then chores, social studies, then help with a younger sibling, writing, then reading aloud with his mom, science, then more chores. Ray and I wrote down just about everything that was said in these workshops--and came home and applied as much as we could. We wanted a life like that for our children.

About that same time, some friends from church introduced us to Bill Gothard's Institute in Basic Life Principles seminar.[6] We

•Lisa went to high school the next year, and did much better in a larger school with a stronger special education program.

attended the Basic Seminar, then the Advanced Seminar. These were especially life-changing for us as we came to understand so much about our past, about living a character-filled life, about relationships, and much more.

BIBLICAL MODELS FOR TEACHING

When You Lie Down, When You Rise Up, When You Sit Down, When You Walk by the Way

Fast forward several years later. We had five children ten and under, and we were homeschooling, of course. We had used unit studies from the beginning--some I created, as well as KONOS[7] (a character-based unit study program). We loved homeschooling! We applied as many things as we could to our homeschool--trying to live a relational homeschooling life, but something was still missing. We continued to find ourselves putting out fires more than relating to our kids. In many ways, we still lived a life that was filled with rules and regulations more than relationship and had not found that transition from discipline and chastisement to heart-training.

Then we moved an hour away from our families--and we were immersed in a homeschool environment. We lived near a county line in which one county had a homeschooling group of thirty families and the other had one with fifty families. We were in homeschool heaven! After attending homeschooling meetings and state conventions, we learned more about what our "homeschool verse" in Deuteronomy meant: "You shall love the Lord your God with all your heart, with all your soul, and with all your strength. And these words which I command you today shall be in your heart. You shall teach them diligently to your children, and shall talk of them when you sit in your house, when you walk by the way, when you lie down, and when you rise up. You shall bind them as a sign on your hand, and they shall be as frontlets between your eyes" Deuteronomy 6: 5-8 (NKJV).[8]

It wasn't long before we came to understand that we were supposed to teach our children what we ourselves had in our hearts. Homeschooling was 24/7. It wasn't an approach to education. It was a lifestyle.

Add to Your Faith, Virtue; and to Your Virtue, Knowledge

A couple of years later, we began using a homeschooling curriculum (the Advanced Training Institute's unit study approach) that helped us focus even more on the most effective order for our homeschool. We learned in I Peter that Christians are to begin with faith, then add virtue (character), then knowledge: "But also for this very reason, giving all diligence, add to your faith virtue, to virtue knowledge" (II Peter 1:5 NKJV).[9] This became the basis for our homeschooling---our curriculum choices, the time we spent on each subject, and even our daily schedule. (See our sequel, *Ages and Stages of the Well-Trained Heart*, for more information about scheduling school with the WTH approach.)

This verse helped us reduce the emphasis on academics and increase the emphasis on character; however, many of us in this curriculum still struggled because we continued to focus on following rules with our children. Yes, we wanted to teach our children character first. Yes, we wanted God's Word to be supreme. Yes, we wanted academics to have its proper place, but we still felt that we were living a homeschooling lifestyle with a running list of do's and don't's--many of which we did not have reasons for. Our children loved us and trusted us, and they wanted us to have their hearts, and we desperately wanted their hearts, but we still parented so much out of fear--fear that our kids would disappoint us, fear that they would do something off the "do not do" list, like listen to the wrong music, wear the wrong clothing, or watch the wrong movie.

The Rest of the Story...

The rest of the story is long...longer than even this story up to this point. You can learn more about our transition from rules to relationship in the chapter entitled, "All I Really Needed to Know I Learned From Debate" (Part II of our journey). Suffice it to say that we learned that we needed to do many things to have the heart approach we desired in our homeschool: (1) talk--without expectations or judgment; (2) know what we believe and why; (3) explain the why's to our kids--especially our teens--and be willing to hear their views on them; (4) live a life that we wanted them to live; (5) yield our rights to time, hobbies, and things in order to spend the energy, resources, and money on our children; and much more.

WE HAD AN APPROACH

A Better Way

About ten years ago, when Joshua was fourteen, we began to realize that God had given us an approach to homeschooling, a lifestyle that yielded far greater results than the norm. It began with us not wanting our children to be away. We were no longer just fearful of the influence of others--we truly wanted to be the influencers of our children. We didn't want to keep them from others just to protect them (though that is part of it, of course), but we *wanted* to be with them. Training them, spending time with them, loving them, growing with them--these were our heart cries.

Next, we discovered that our kids actually did a lot better socially, emotionally, and spiritually if they spent more time with us than with their peers. We quit putting them into so many clubs, organizations, and activities, and substituted ourselves instead (more on this in "Let It Begin With Me"). And they were doing great! We discovered that their spending more time with us and less time with peers resulted in better character and stronger faith. We found that neither we, nor they, even missed the other activities and excessive interactions.

A Different Way

Then we came to realize that this approach was vastly different than many homeschooling parents'. After our kids were with other kids in small group or hospitality times in our, home, we would ask them questions about the other kids and their relationships with their parents and siblings. Our children would tell us various things about the families, then when we commented that a family sounded a lot like ours, the kids would correct us. They weren't sure what the differences were, but they knew there were differences in the way they were being raised and the way others were. Sometimes it would come out in little details like, "Their dad doesn't spend his evenings with them like Dad does with us" or "Their mom doesn't talk to them like you do to us." They weren't sure exactly why a family was different than ours. They just sensed it was something. And we knew that this heart-training approach was the reason.

At our homeschooling group's graduations, the parents and the students get a chance to speak for a couple of minutes. Many times the parents have talked about the kids' academic achievements: high SAT scores, college credits already earned, outstanding grade point averages, and prestigious scholarships. The students have often talked about their parents' patience with them through the tough years they had put them through, their mom as their teacher and their dad as their principal, and how homeschooling had prepared them to go to college, etc. While none of that is wrong, and our children had many college credits, high scores, and outstanding academic achievements as well, it has been interesting to us that our prepared notes included information about our kids' character--their selflessness in serving their family, their love and gentleness towards their younger siblings, their service to God and others.

Our children didn't mention much about the academic success we had helped them achieve either; they didn't call Dad their principal and Mom their teacher. They described the love and help provided to them by their siblings and parents; they described Dad and Mom both as their teachers of many, many things. They detailed their dad's selflessness in leaving his fulfilling career to take a lesser job to spend time with them. And we realized we had an approach to homeschooling--and life--that could truly make an eternal difference in our children. These are things of the heart. We had an approach--it was the well-trained heart approach.

"Our Journey to the Center of the Heart"
Discussion/Application Questions
-- Chapter 2 --

1. Do you put knowledge ahead of heart training? How can you change your focus to be more on eternal things?
2. What relational influences have you had in your Christian life? How can the mentoring that you received from others be applied to the mentoring of your teens and young adults?
3. Do you find yourself placing measureable, praise-able things above the more long-term, less measurable things? How can you focus more on the long-term things?
4. What can you say to your children to let them know that you want to value heart things over surface things?
5. Do you find yourself parenting with a more authoritarian, you-will-do-what-I-say-because-I-say-so approach? How can you balance obedience and submission training with more gentleness and kindness in approaching your young children?
6. Do you feel deep gratitude for those homeschooling pioneers who went before you and taught you the how-to's of homeschooling? Discuss ways that you can do that for new homeschoolers in your life.
7. Does your curriculum have a relational, heart-training feel to it or is it all about academics? If it is strongly academically-oriented, what can you add to your homeschool to bring in more heart-training?
8. How would your children respond to the chocolate milk scenario faced by the Coriell's? Do your children see you obeying God and authorities at all times, or do they see you trying to outsmart authorities (speeding, tax returns, etc.)?
9. How do you apply Deuteronomy 6:5-8 to your family? Do you seek to have God and his ways in your heart first? In what ways do you try to share with your children what you have in your heart throughout the day and night?

THREE

All I Really Need to Know I Learned From Debate

How We Discovered the Well-Trained Heart Approach Part II of II

LOVE AND REASONS

In the previous chapter, I left off with the facts that we were introduced to homeschooling in a relational way. Terry and Esa Everroad, Dr. Raymond Moore, Gregg Harris, the Coriell's, and Bill Gothard all taught us about homeschooling as a lifestyle--one in which academics is a part of it--but only a part. Then we went on to realize that the Bible also gave us some instructions on teaching God's Word to our children and ordering our lives so that temporal things are last on the list, and we applied those things to our homeschool. Next, we found that this type of heart-training required more than just keeping our children away from negative influences. We had to be their primary influencers. Then we discovered that if we took the time, energy, patience, and money that was needed to get into our kids' hearts, it would result in something greater than merely home "educating" them.

This chapter is titled "All I Really Need to Know I Learned From Debate." Now, obviously, that isn't completely true, but ever since I was in college and read the book *All I Really Need to Know I Learned in Kindergarten*,[1] I have wanted to use a spin off of that title somewhere, so here it is! While I didn't actually learn everything I need to know from debate, I do have debate to thank for teaching me how to think--and for helping me teach my children how to think.

Love Was the Rule

I look back on the time when our three oldest children began entering their teen years, and it seems a miracle that we were able to keep their hearts. I know that there were some key experiences during that time that held us together so closely, in spite of our tendency to not always think when making rules and guidelines.

The most significant thing that kept our children true to us during that time was love. More than anything else, love ruled our home. We might have had some wacko rules, many of which had no logical basis. We might have taken away a lot of things from them that other kids got to do or have (and continue to do so). But we always loved unselfishly. We loved them enough to do whatever it took to stay close to them.

Paul's declaration about ruling with love is what made those years successful in spite of not knowing what we were doing! In Philemon 1: 8-9, Paul told the people that he could have forced them to do what he wanted them to do (which is how some parents handle things), but instead he wanted to love them into doing what he asked: "...although in Christ I could be bold and order you to do what you ought to do, yet I appeal to you on the basis of love" (NKJV).[2]

When we appeal to our children on the basis of love--even if we do not have it all figured out ourselves yet--their response is completely different than if we appeal to them with unlimited, tyrannical authority.

Give Children the Reason

As indicated many other places in this book, we firmly believe in giving children the reasons for our decisions. Now, we think our children should obey and respect us regardless of whether they know the reason or not, but the reason should be given, so that they are able to apply that reason later to other questions and situations they might encounter, and so that they do not become exasperated with us.

However, as our two oldest children entered the teen years, our reasons quit holding up so well. Oh, Joshua and Kayla still did what we wanted them to do, almost entirely. They still followed our rules and wishes for them, but they were often not satisfied with our reasons.

Our two first-born children are intellectually gifted. They enjoy logic and reasoning. I, on the other hand, am average intellectually and much more emotional in nature. Ray is intellectually gifted but unusually emotional and intimate too. I say this to help you understand that when we gave our children reasons for our rules or explained why we believe as we do, I relied on emotional and relational answers. (This isn't all bad, but those answers do not always hold up when talking to intellectual young people). Ray, on the other hand, relied on both emotion and logic. Regardless of our approach, we soon discovered that many of our reasons for our rules and lifestyle choices made little sense. We did many things because we heard them at conventions, church, or home-schooling meetings.

So, around the time that Joshua was fifteen and Kayla was twelve, they suggested that we study different things together and decide what we believe, rather than just following what someone told us we should believe. And we agreed with them. So we took many topics that were unclear to us--the church, the Holy Spirit, women's roles in the church, music, clothing, and modesty--and began to study them together, using the Bible as our basis, rather than a workbook from a seminar or a handout from a convention.

Many of our findings surprised us. Some of our "rules" were based on one verse in the Bible, an Old Testament law that we inconsistently followed. Some of our beliefs were narrow, not at all like Jesus taught. Many were man-made. They sounded "good," so even though they were man-made, we followed them. These study times helped us solidify our beliefs and helped us give our children the reason for many things we held to.

CONVICTIONS AND BELIEFS

Joining Debate

About that time, a gal in our homeschooling group started a speech and debate class. The next year we found ourselves teaching it and leading it and learning right along with the students how to think, find evidence, apply evidence to arguments, and so much more. We taught and coached speech and debate for seven years (and continue to teach speech and debate today).

In summary, when a student debates (at least in the homeschooling league we were in[3]), he prepares a case for a certain topic (i.e. tax laws should be changed). He chooses a certain aspect or two that he wants to change in that topic and prepares a presentation for that--an opening, harms (things the current tax law is causing), changes (things that will correct the harms), and a closing. (There is more to it than that, but for our purposes here, I'll keep it brief.)

In order to make his case, the student uses many things--logic (if this change were made, logically these things would result), appeal to emotions (someone is being hurt by the current system), and evidence (influential people saying that the change would help, other laws that are similar that have helped, statistics showing how the change would help, etc.). Now, a student must be logical, have evidence, be articulate, be on the defensive, etc., in order to win a debate (much like a lawyer winning a courtroom case).

Joshua and Kayla were in the height of their glory when they were debating. They loved the whole process--the logic, the research, the making of arguments, the thinking required to get an answer, etc. And somehow, throughout the first couple of years in debate, we started to see the importance of evidence for our reasons, logic for our rules, and researching even more what we truly believed.

Which Came First? The Conviction or the Reason?

In our first year or two of debate, we had the privilege of attending the national debate and speech tournament, the goal of most every NCFCA speech and debate student. During this particular tournament, Christy Farris Shipe[4] (daughter of Michael Farris, founder of Home School Legal Defense[5]) spoke. Christy initiated the national homeschool debate league when she was a college student, so we have her to thank for much of our debate training (and her father to thank for preserving our freedoms to homeschool).

Anyway, I do not remember all of what Christy's speech was about as she addressed the entire group of hundreds of debaters and their families, but I do remember one thing. Paraphrased from my memory of that night, she said, *We have to get to the point where we quit deciding what we believe, then looking for verses to back up that belief. It should be the other way around. We should read the Bible, find verses that convict us of something, then make our belief based on those verses--not come up with a belief, then find the verses that we want to use to substantiate that belief.*

Wow! That is what I had been doing my entire life as a Christian parent. I heard or read something that sounded like a good idea. Then I discovered that there were isolated verses that could be used to "prove" my idea or belief (which really wasn't my idea or belief anyway). This was truly groundbreaking in my life, another stepping stone to understanding what I believe and why--and in being able to pass on my beliefs to my children.

Our Children Should Be Able to Verbalize Their Beliefs

From that experience, we began teaching our children more and more about our beliefs, and through speech and debate, learned the value of articulating those beliefs. We wanted our children to know what they believed well enough that they not only knew it, but they could tell others. We didn't want them just quoting what we told them or what a book said, but we wanted them to know it for themselves.

An example of this lies in an embarrassing story about me related to football. I am not well-versed in football. If we are somewhere with a television on and football (or nearly any sport, really) is playing, I tune it out to the point that I do not even know what sport is being shown on the screen.

However, I was raised with football. My older brother played football all of his high school years. I cheered for football for three years in junior high and high school. My younger brother played football in high school, then in college. As an adult, he has coached high school football and semi-pro football. So it is not like I haven't had extensive exposure to the sport.

But for some reason, I never paid attention to the rules--like how you score, what a quarterback is--those important details of the game. Well, several years ago, our family was at a game that my brother was coaching when I accidentally watched the game for a few minutes. Someone scored, but he didn't run underneath that goal thingy. I leaned over to my son and asked why they counted the points when he didn't run under the thingy. My son laughed and laughed, and so has my entire family since then. I truly did not know that the player did not have to run directly underneath the goal post to score.

I had been immersed in football from childhood. I had cheered, "First and ten and do it again!" (Even though I had no idea what that meant.) I yelled and hollered for them to sack the quarterback (whoever he is). Yet in spite of being immersed in it and even being able to quote back words I had heard (cheers), I didn't actually know about football myself.

The same thing can happen to our children. They can live immersed in the Christian life in our homes for years and years. We can get them to repeat the right words to us---that Jesus died on the cross, that he rose again, that you must be born again, that you should follow the ten commandments, and so forth. Yet, in spite of that immersion and those robotic words, if we do not get them involved in the faith for themselves, teach them why they believe what they do, help them to comprehend the faith well enough to reiterate it themselves (not just quoting us), then it will not truly be theirs--any more than the game of football was mine.

DEBATE AND STANDARDS

Debate Causing Child to Argue

Many people introduced to debate worry that their teen will become even more argumentative if he learns how to debate. There is some truth in that. If your child argues with you about rules and your family's beliefs, debate may make him argue even more - with more logic and evidence!

However, if your child is not argumentative to begin with, debate will not make him argumentative toward you. Our experience has been that debate helped us learn to think better--and helped us teach our children to think better. Yes, our children who were already more prone to arguing did argue more, but we just forbade them from "using debate" on us at first.

Arguing is not always a negative thing--when done with character. Creationists often debate evolutionists. Politicians debate each other. And your children, more than likely, debate other children (especially those who are being raised differently than they are).

How much better to give your students the tools needed to debate properly, reasonably, and biblically than to have your child give a "little Pharisee" response that is common among untrained, argumentative young people.

When a child is questioned about his standards, and he responds with shallow answers like *We don't believe in that* or *My parents don't like that* or *That's bad*--with no logic, evidence, or reasons, he is truly unprepared *to give an answer*: "But in your hearts set apart Christ as Lord. *Always be prepared to give an answer to everyone who asks you to give the reason for the hope that you have.* But do this with gentleness and respect" (I Peter 3:15 NIV).[6]

We must not send our youth out unprepared. Just telling them "because I said so," or "the Bible says not to," (where does it say this?) is not preparing them. It might make us feel superior to have that sort of power, but it is truly not preparing our young people.

God and the Because-I-Told-You-So Approach

It is interesting to note that when we discussed many of these issues with Joshua while preparing this book, he said that the reason he did what we wanted him to do (outside of love) during our less-than-rational-rule-time is because no matter what rule we made, what standard we expected, or what behavior we demanded, we always listened to him. He said that even if we did not change the rule or expected result, we still let him talk and let him disagree with us. He noted that it didn't matter if we followed his suggestions, just the fact that we were listening to him made all the difference in the world. According to him, we did not give him freedom to do as he pleased when he disagreed with something, but we did give him intellectual freedom--the freedom to think and to question us.

That leads us to more deeply ponder God's approach to us. We parents can be so quick to answer our children with "because I told you so." And yet, God rarely does that. Yes, there are times when he asked difficult things without any explanation (like in the case of Abraham sacrificing Isaac[7]), but more often than not, he does not say "I told you so." He lets us pray and plead our requests before him. He is not a far off, "I told you so" God--and we should not be far off, "I told you so" parents either.

Debate vs Service

So we were into speech and debate in a big way. It prepared our four oldest children to minister and serve eloquently, logically, and reasonably. However, as the years went by, debate began to feel more like an organized school program rather than a homeschooling program. We became uncomfortable with the lengthy, expensive, and exclusive (to the rest of the family) tournaments. When the league was smaller and newer, we always went as a family, worked together to serve others at the tournament, etc. As the league grew, the competition also grew, which caused some parents to act like unruly little league parents rather than loving homeschooling parents. Winning became too important to many.

Then one weekend in the spring of 2006, I was at a tournament with Jonathan and Kara when I realized in full the place that speech and debate had in our lives: preparing for service. At that particular tournament, I was being interviewed at the debate site for a magazine article about our ministry; Ray and Jacob were speaking at a homeschooling convention a few hours from home; Joshua, Lisa, and Josiah were speaking at a convention several hours from home; Kayla was back home teaching public speaking skills to some of the young adult leaders at church; Cami was back home teaching a pre-teen group about serving your family when you are young. And I looked around at the tournament with gratitude and realized that this truly had prepared our children for many things--but it should not become an end in itself.

We had thought that all of our children would compete in speech and debate for all of their junior high and high school years. Competition made them stronger speakers, better researchers, more logical thinkers, and more outstanding leaders. But competition also has its downsides. We became uncomfortable with the amount of time and effort that went into competition as we wanted them to use their time for service, too.

Now, we are still avid speech and debate fans. We continue to teach speech and debate classes in a few locations in Indiana and Ohio every year. However, our competitive years are not as extensive. Jonathan and Kara have already competed for two and four years, respectively. Now they are involved in drama ministry for a season. Our two youngest boys will more than likely compete at some time--as "iron sharpens iron"--but not for all of their junior high and high school years--and never to the exclusion of serving others. And not if we see winning debate as becoming too important to them.

So, we have come full circle. Being extensively involved in debate helped us learn to think. And in thinking more consistently about time and service, debate helped us to see that competing full time every year is probably not in the best interest of our children. Competition and worthwhile educational activities have their place in the well-trained heart homeschool, but never to the exclusion of service--which is our purpose for being here.

"All I Really Need to Know I Learned From Debate"
Discussion/Application Questions
-- Chapter 3 --

1. When you do not "have it all figured out" with your children, do you appeal to them in love? Do you admit that you don't know the answer either, but you want them to trust you in the meantime?
2. What areas or rules do you have that might not be fully understood? What about areas that your children legitimately question? Are you willing to study these with your children?
3. What do you think about the evidence and logic for rules? Do you feel the "because I told you so" approach rising within you when you think about providing answers to your children? How does the "because I told you so" approach compare to how God treats us?
4. Think about the convictions and lifestyle "rules" you have for yourself and your children. Which came first, the rule or the verse? Have you picked and chosen rules and ideals when you have heard them presented--and then added verses that seemed to apply?
5. If your children try to discuss or question things respectfully, do you shut them off immediately? How can you listen to your children more fully when they question family rules?
6. Do you see the importance of preparing your children to defend what they believe?
7. How do you feel about activities (even "good" ones like debate or music) over service? Do you have the view that your children's young adult years are for "playing" or "taking part in activities" as more important than using their time to serve God and others or be involved in ministry? If so, how do you think this affects them now, and how will it affect them in the future?

FOUR

Bible Heart Beat

What the Bible Says About Heart Training

WHAT ABOUT THE HEART?

The Bible has a lot to say about the heart, heart training, parenting, children, and education. Over and over, we are told about the condition of our hearts and how to guard them. Scripture also points out that parents can actually have their child's heart to guard and train until the child is ready to guard and train it for himself.

The Heart Is the Center of a Person

In the Bible, the *heart* is often used interchangeably with the word *soul*. Both of them are used to denote the inner part; the seat of emotion; the seat of spirituality. Of course, contemporary ways of looking at the heart also indicate that it is the essence of who we are. We say that we love "with all of our hearts." We suggest that a heart (a person's very being) can be so broken that it wills the body to no longer live, as in when a lifetime mate dies and shortly thereafter the spouse also passes. We indicate that we believe something with "our heart of hearts"--the very center of ourselves.

The Heart Is Wicked

Over and over in Scripture we are reminded that we are all born sinners. That we (including our children) are born with sin natures. So one of the first things we need to understand about the heart as we train our children is that it is wicked: "The heart is deceitful above all things, And desperately wicked; Who can know it?" Jeremiah 17:9 (NKJV).[1] Our children, just like us, need their hearts cleansed and changed. They need a Savior.

Of course, the wickedness in our hearts can be removed by the blood of Christ. However, wickedness continues to seep into our hearts because of our sin natures, and we continually need a Savior to remove the wickedness from our hearts. And so do our children.

The Heart Can Be Deceived

In our society we often use the phrase "love is blind" to refer to someone being deceived by someone else, as in getting involved in a relationship that might not be good for that person. "Love is blind" means that someone is so enamored with another person that he or she can not see clearly what the person is really like or how he or she could be damaged by a relationship with that person. In essence, we are saying that the heart is "deceived."

Of course, like most modern takes on heart conditions, the Bible has already warned us of the heart's tendency to be deceived. In

Deuteronomy, we are told that our hearts can be deceived and that when they are, we will often turn away from God to other gods: "Take heed to yourselves, lest your heart be deceived, and you turn aside and serve other gods and worship them" Deuteronomy 11:16 (NKJV).[2]

If our "mature," adult hearts are easily deceived, how much more can immature, vulnerable, tender hearts be deceived? We see this over and over when parents caution a child about friends who are negatively influencing him, and the child simply does not discern it. We see this over and over when parents desire for a young person not to be in a harmful relationship with someone of the opposite gender, and the young person is sure that there is no harm present. We see this over and over when parents warn their son not to read or view potentially dangerous material, but the son is sure he will not be affected by that material. In all of these instances, the heart has been deceived, and it is extremely difficult to penetrate that deceived heart with truth.

The Heart Is Often Revealed in Our Speech

In Matthew, Jesus says that we speak about what we have in our hearts: "You brood of snakes! How could evil men like you speak what is good and right? For whatever is in your heart determines what you say" Matthew 12:34 (NLT).[3]

We all know that we often speak without thinking. The Bible also tells us to listen more than we speak, to think before we speak, to weigh our words before we speak. Oftentimes, when we speak without thinking, we are speaking heart words. We are revealing what is in our hearts.

This is one reason that we believe so strongly that we must allow vast amounts of time to get into our children's hearts. We must get in a position with them that they are comfortable talking to us--that they do not withhold confiding in us because of our judgment or disapproval of them. And as we talk and share in our children's lives, many heart things will spill forth--the abundance of the heart will often be revealed through intense and frequent communication with our children.

The Heart Has the Capacity to Love Deeply

Even though the heart is described as wicked and easily deceived, it is also noted throughout the Bible that it has the capacity to love deeply, as indicated in verses about loving God with all of our hearts. Because the heart can love and feel so deeply, it is easily hurt.

Contemporary ways of looking at the heart are based on the fact that the heart can love and feel so thoroughly. Because of its capacity for love, we often say that the heart can be *broken*, *trampled*, *wounded*, *pierced*, *softened*, *hardened*, *kept*, *held*, *preserved*, *given away*, *protected*, *cherished*, and so on. It is truly a bottomless vessel of emotion and feeling.

The Heart Must Be Prepared or "Set" to Seek God

The Bible tells us that when Rehoboam led Israel, he forsook the law of God, as did the entire nation along with him. That in itself is not too amazing since many Old Testament leaders acted similarly to him. The key to his unfaithfulness and evil is found in II Chronicles 12:14--"And he did evil, for he did not set his heart to seek the Lord" (NJKV).[4] The reason Rehoboam's life and verse fourteen are significant to our heart study is that both of them indicate that (1) the heart has the capacity for wickedness and (2) the heart can be "set" or "prepared" to seek the Lord. Thus, there is something that the owner of the heart must do in order to seek God.

How does one "set" his heart to seek the Lord? There are many ways one can set his heart to seek the Lord (through yielding, prayer, introspection, repentance, worship, etc.), but it is significant to note that a young person seldom sets his heart to seek the Lord (and keeps it set throughout his life) without having his heart protected and trained in how to do so. This is evidenced by the myriad statistics (see Barna research[5]) showing the small percentage of young people who remain faithful to God all through their youth and into adulthood (i.e. not those who "come back to God" later as adults).

It seems that Rehoboam was significantly influenced by the evil around him. Nobody had held his heart for him, protected it, poured into it. Nobody had trained him in how to "set" his heart for God.

The Heart Can Be Turned Away From One Thing and Towards Another

When our older children were younger, we claimed Malachi 4:6 as the basis for the fact that our children's hearts would be turned to us and our hearts to them: "And he will turn the hearts of the fathers to the children. And the hearts of the children to their fathers. Lest I come and strike the earth with a curse" Malachi 4:6 (NKJV).[6]

Now we understand that this verse is not a promise in that capacity, but it is an indication that the heart *can* be turned from one thing to another thing--and that the parents' hearts can be turned to their children and vice versa. The turning suggested in Malachi 4:6 refers to a returning, a bringing back. This gives us hope that our children's hearts can be turned back to us--even if they are turned away from us now.

The turning described in this verse is done by the Lord. Many wayward sons and daughters have been turned back to their parents and to their parents' God by the prayers of a mother or grandmother. This verse suggests to us that God can turn those hearts back--and that we should appeal to him to do so.

The Heart Can Be Controlled by Its Owner

There are many verses that tell us to control our hearts, to keep them from being deceived, to keep them from evil, to set them towards God, and so forth. These passages indicate to us that we, as adults, can control our hearts. We can protect them. We can keep them from evil.

Psalm 131:2 tells of how we can quiet and control our souls just like a child who is weaned: "But I have stilled and quieted my soul; like a weaned child with its mother, like a weaned child is my soul within me" (Psalms 131:2 NIV).[7]

For a long time, I have had an interest in this verse in connection with when our children are ready to be weaned from the breast, as well as when our children's behavior should begin changing from childishness to responsibility. For our purposes here, it tells me that there is a time in a child's life that comes gradually, like a child being weaned, in which he is capable of quieting his own soul, his own heart. However, this ability to quiet one's soul comes later in a child's life--much like I Corinthians 13 says, "When I was a child, I talked like a child, I thought like a child, I reasoned like a child. When I became a man, I put childish ways behind me" (NIV).[8]

We believe the heart can eventually be controlled by the child as he enters adulthood--a little at a time. However, we also believe that the Bible encourages us to gain our child's heart while he is younger because he needs to be protected by us until he is prepared to take care of his heart himself.

The Heart Can Be Given Away

Because the heart is so fragile and so easily broken, and because children are foolish, Scripture suggests in various places that children give their hearts to their parents. Why? Could it be because this fragile, crucial seat of emotion within our child could be protected from much hurt if the parents hold and protect it rather than exposing it to pain and evil before the child is ready to protect it himself? We believe so.

Proverbs 23:26 says, "My son, give me thine heart, And let thine eyes observe my ways" (NKJV).[9] The word *son* here may refer to *young* men, as well as both genders of offspring, male and female.

Solomon, the wisest man who ever lived, and the one who told us over and over again to chastise, use the rod, discipline, and rebuke our children, also told his child that a son (or daughter) should give his heart to his father (or mother)--*then watch how the parent lives*. That is both frightening and overwhelming.

How many of us are in a position spiritually to tell our child, "Give me your heart. I will hold it for you and protect it for you. Then you watch how I live, so that when I give your heart back to you, you will know how to live and what to do with it"? And yet this is the advice to parents from the wisest man who ever lived.

The Heart Can Be Trained

Proverbs 22:15 is often cited for proof that we should discipline our children: "Foolishness is bound up in the heart of a child; The rod of correction will drive it far from him" Proverbs 22:15 (NKJV).[10] We agree that it does indicate a child's foolish condition and that it gives an antidote for that condition. However, we believe it tells us even more than that.

This, along with other verses about how the heart can be trained, turned, held, and instructed, lead us to understand that once a parent has a child's heart, training can take place more easily. We do not gain our children's hearts so that we can control the children; we gain their hearts so that we can pour into their lives the precious truths that God has given us to pour. Without their giving of their hearts to us, no pouring takes place. Without the pouring in, the relationship, interaction, and intimacy required for heart training will not take place.

So What About the Heart?

So...in summary, we believe that the heart is wicked. That we often speak about what we have in our hearts--whether we mean to or not. That the heart can be trained--especially when the parent has the heart. That the heart can be given away--and that if we train our child properly when he is younger, we have a good chance of being the one that he gives his heart to. We believe that the heart can be turned back to parents and God--even when it is turned away. And that our goal in parenting is to secure, protect, and train our children's hearts--until they are ready to quiet, control, and protect their hearts themselves.

TWO STORIES OF THE HEART

We know of two poignant examples of families and children's hearts. While we believe there are many aspects to a child's turning away from God and his parents and a child staying true to God and his parents, these two examples point to definite actions on the parents' and children's parts that influenced the turning away and remaining true that we feel will give you a good look at some of the heart aspects detailed in this chapter (and throughout this book).

Lost Heart

We know of a mother and father who secured their son's heart early on, but eventually lost it through not fully understanding the dangers to the heart of a young man--and through choosing to make their son "happy" rather than "holy." During Sam's preschool days, his parents did many of the things that we feel cause a child to be tender, give his heart to his parents, submit to their authority, etc. They disciplined him for rebellion and disobedience, and they made him endure the consequences of poor character. They protected him from negative influences, keeping him with them more than with peers and making sure he was not in environments that were emotionally and physically dangerous. They taught him the Bible and godly character both at home and through church. They spent a lot of time with him, both in fun and in learning, and they did not indulge him in too many frivolities or spoil him with so many gizmos and gadgets that their teaching and love were drowned out. They talked to him all the time, training him during "teachable moments" and so on.

At first, Sam went to elementary school, but his parents (as well as Sam) desired for him to become a missionary and wanted to train him more in Bible and character than going to school would allow them, both in terms of time and influences. Thus, he was homeschooled from upper junior high through high school. During junior high, they continued in the protection and training with which they began. Their home was a fun place to be, and the entire family enjoyed being there. Mom and Dad talked continuously to their son, and it was clear that somewhere between childhood and adolescence, Sam gave his heart to his parents to protect and train.

Then these parents began letting their guard down. It started with all season, demanding sports programs, which resulted in constant interaction with peers of all faiths--and no faiths. Sam's parents falsely believed that this would be a good thing--that Sam would influence these young people more than they would influence him. However, Sam was not ready at such a young age and such a tender time in his heart training to take on this monumental task (one that many adults are not even prepared for). Instead, he discovered freedom and fun in hanging out with friends more than with his parents. Before the family knew it, Sam began taking his heart back from his parents a little at a time--and giving it to his peers. His character began resembling that of his peers, as noted in unusual (for Sam) bahaviors, such as disrespect for adults, making fun of the weak, irresponsibility, lack of diligence, and so on.

Now Sam was gone from home as much or more than he was home. Heart training was nearly non-existent as his life and his parents' lives now revolved around activities rather than family. His relationships with his siblings changed significantly as they no longer had Sam as their "best friend."

Next, Sam decided he wanted to earn money to get a vehicle. His parents saw wisdom in this as they would not have to drive him around so much if he had his own car. Sam began working in a fast-food restaurant in town, after his school work was done and his sports activities were over, at first. Gradually, however, Sam skipped school work more and more, beginning with Bible, in order to work more daytime hours and play more in the evenings. More negative influences were encountered at work, and when his parents tried to question him about these influences and about Sam's heart's condition, he refused to talk to them.

By now, Sam's parents had very little of his heart in their possession at all--and the part they barely clung to was hardly teachable anyway. It was busy, distracted, and seeking for more fun and more pleasure day by day. He and his parents seldom talked anymore, in part because they didn't have time to talk and in part because Sam was hiding evil in his heart and did not want to reveal this to his parents.

The ending to this story is not happy. Sam eventually ran off and married a non-Christian, against his parents' wishes. Years passed, and, thankfully, Sam and his bride came back to the Lord and back to his parents' home for reconciliation, but much of the damage was irrevocable. His father was bitter towards him for all of the hurt he had caused the family. The younger siblings all floundered in ways similar to Sam as their parents lost the confidence and drive to try anymore. Sam had exposed his fragile heart to all kinds of negative influences and evil while it was unprotected by his parents. While he came back to God, and thankfully, walked with God in his adult years, he never did truly great things for God because he spent much of his adulthood trying to fill the holes and mend the broken parts of his unguarded heart.

Secured Heart

The second story is that of a secured heart. Like Sam's parents, "Lindsay's" parents began early in the heart training of their daughter. They taught Lindsay God's Word and godly character daily and trained her in diligence and responsibility as she grew from preschool into elementary school. They protected her from negative influences and gave up their hobbies, interests, and time to be her primary influencers. She, along with her younger brothers, enjoyed fun family times as well as training times. They were with peers in protected environments, so they seldom heard how "rough" they had it that they were not allowed the extensive "peer time" that other kids their age had.

As Lindsay grew into junior high, her parents encouraged her to use her time to serve others. She got so busy with school, helping young families with their small children, teaching kids at church, and writing a character-based newsletter for young girls that she didn't notice all of the "fun" she was missing by not running around with peers all the time.

Lindsay and her parents had special relationships since Lindsay gave her heart to her parents. They protected it and trained it--and gave of themselves to replace the things they "took" from her (compared to what her peers had and did). Lindsay grew in the godly characteristics of kindness, empathy, diligence, responsibility, love, and more in this environment. Her heart did not long for what she didn't have because it was being protected by those who loved her more than anyone else ever could.

As Lindsay entered high school, she found more and more ways to serve God and others. She and two friends held two week-end long summer training camps for teen girls at a local state park. They spent dozens of hours writing the Bible lessons, planning the meals and crafts, securing the supplies and grounds, etc. They worked extra jobs to earn the money needed to offset the expenses that were not covered by the nominal fees they charged the attendees.

Many nights were spent in heart talks between Lindsay and her parents. She was always free to discuss everything and anything with them because they understood the importance of letting her ask questions, even if they were ones concerning their standards or rules. Lindsay seldom "broke the rules" simply because they were not burdensome to her--she understood the reasons behind them and knew that her parents had her best interest in mind at all times.

When other girls her age were dating around, Lindsay knew what she wanted in a future mate--and knew that it would not be obtained by trying out different boyfriends during her teen years. She was willing to wait for the marriage she dreamed of because she observed her parents' marriage--and knew it was worth the wait.

After high school, Lindsay followed the advice of her parents and took a year off from school before making a decision on which direction she would head (education, internship, ministry, etc.). During that time she took distance learning classes at home from a local college.

Then it happened. A year after her high school graduation, Lindsay went to a Christian conference with her brother. As she met the challenge to hike to the top of her first mountain in Colorado, she met the man of her dreams. In a whirlwind year and a half, this young man asked her father if he could court her; they had a long-distance courtship; and they married, with both parents' blessings and both of their hearts intact.

Complete Disasters and Perfect Endings

Obviously, things do not always go so terribly as they did with Sam when a heart is not held by the parents. Likewise, things do not always go as perfectly as they did for Lindsay when the heart is secured by Mom and Dad (though they are both true stories). These are just two extreme examples of what can happen when Christian parents do and do not get their child's heart--and train it and keep it until the child is ready to protect and train the heart himself. Heart holding and protecting is worth the effort. It is the basis of the relational approach to parenting. It is the beginning of the well-trained heart.

"Bible Heart Beat"
Discussion/Application Questions
-- Chapter 4 --

1. Consider verses that you misuse to tell others what to do, like in the case of Deuteronomy 6:5 and 6. Do you still think that those verses (whatever yours might be) are commands to do something other than the context in which they were used?
2. Can you recount any times recently in which one of your children spoke out of the abundance of his heart? Were you willing to listen, even if it wasn't what you wanted to hear? Can you listen to the hearts of your children more fully?
3. What do you think the heart's capacity to love deeply has to do with contemporary terminology for conditions of the heart--broken, pierced, stolen, etc.?
4. Do you think Solomon's words to his son to give his father his heart apply to us today? If so, how can you work towards gaining your child's heart?
5. More importantly, what can you do in your own life to be able to say what Solomon said: "...watch how I live, so that when I give your heart back to you, you will know how to live and what to do with it"?
6. What steps are you taking with the various ages of children to help them turn their hearts to their parents--instead of towards peers?
7. When do you think a child can quiet his soul or heart himself? How do the verses about quieting your soul and thinking like a child apply to the youth culture today in which young people do not control their hearts and lives?
8. Do you desire to have your children's hearts so that you can control them or so that you can pour good things into them--the things you already have in your own life?

FIVE

Let It Begin With Me

The Well-Trained Heart Begins With Mom and Dad

As mentioned in the first chapter of this book, heart training can only be accomplished in our children when we ourselves have well-trained hearts. It starts with each parent individually yielded to God and then to each other. No, you do not have to have a perfect marriage to have well-trained hearts in your children--just a mutually submissive, loving, humble one. Again, it is about not asking our children to be what we are not able or willing to be ourselves.

HAPPY MOM, KIND DAD

If Mama Ain't Happy

There is an old saying that goes "If Mama ain't happy, ain't nobody happy." Most people find that humorous, but I have to ask what God thinks about it. I mean, does God think it is funny that if we

...et our own way, we make everyone around us ...be hilarious if our children made everyone ...e when they were unhappy about some- ...ing did not go their way? Do you see the absurdity ...at?

Yet so many of us mothers, even homeschooling mothers, want things just so in order to be content. We want material items--furnishings, collections, clothes, even homeschooling products--or else we are unhappy. We want order, a noble goal, of course, but if our order becomes disorder, we show our discontentment toward our children. We want good behavior, and when we do not get it, rather than look into our own hearts to see if perhaps we are the cause, we show disfavor and disappointment towards our children. I do not believe there is anything wrong with having nice things. I love order. I definitely think children should obey their parents. But it is our response when those things do not take place that truly matters.

Our children have the potential to become just like us! We mothers, especially, have to guard against discontentment and joylessness. Our children feel rejected and unloved when we act as though everything we have to do for them or with them is drudgery.

A child with a well-trained heart begins with a mother with a well-trained heart. Learn to give your expectations to God--and pray that you can become a joyful mother of children: "He gives the barren woman a home, making her the joyous mother of children. Praise the LORD" Psalms 113:9 (RSV).[1]

Don't Ask Daddy

Fathers are not off the hook in their character and behaviors towards their children. In proper heart training, there should be no "fear" of Daddy. Our children should not be afraid to talk about anything or bring something up with their father for fear he will be unhappy with them or blow up. If mothers are notorious for showing the negative character qualities of discontentment and shallowness in terms of temporal "things," fathers are equally known for being harsh, angry, and abrasive.

Again, the question remains: How can we expect our children to be what we cannot be? How can we expect our children to want relationships with us when we push them away with our disapproval or anger? How can we expect our children to desire to follow a God that we keep at a distance ourselves?

The Bible gives specific instruction for the father to beware that he does not treat his children harshly. It indicates that abrasive behaviors toward our children will cause them to become exasperated.[2] Instead, it calls for fathers to bring their children up in the training and instruction of the Lord, which must be the opposite of this "exasperating" type of training. In our everyday lives, we see that this abrasive behavior and resulting aggravation drive our children away from us.

Whose Heart Is Turned First?

We have already mentioned the verses in Malachi about children's hearts being turned to their parents.[3] But we have often wondered if there is a special significance to the fact that the aforementioned Malachi verse says that God will turn the hearts of the fathers to the children, then the children to the fathers.

Could this be a commentary on the state of fathers' hearts today--that they are often turned away from their children--and need God to turn them toward their children? Could this be the antidote, in part, for children's hearts being turned away from their parents? Could it be that if the father's heart is turned toward his child, the child's heart will more easily turn to the father?

"I'm Just Not Like That"

Many parents, mothers and fathers alike, respond to teaching about intimacy and closeness with their children by saying, "I'm just not made like that." While it is true that we each have varying levels of comfort in our intimacy with others, there are many things in life that we do simply because they are the right things to do and we know God desires for us to do them. In our opinion, being loving to and being intimate with our children are two of those things. When you consider that husbands and wives are to be one, that children are to give us their hearts, that fathers are to treat their children gently so they do not aggravate them, that we are supposed to have godly principles in our hearts then give them to our children, that husbands are to love their wives as Christ loved the church, and on and on, how can we justify our coldness, harshness, or indifference towards our children with "personality" claims?

We could make the same excuse about almost anything: I don't like math, so I'm not going to teach it. I find it hard to do geography, so I'm not putting it in our curriculum. I don't like to wash dishes; it's just not something I am comfortable with, so we will use paper plates for the rest of our lives.

Just like learning anything hard, new, or uncomfortable, learning to be intimate takes time, effort, and sometimes, discomfort. But we can take little steps each day to draw closer to those we love. Intimacy is desperately needed in heart training and worth the effort to develop.

WHO OR WHAT WILL OUR CHILDREN BE LIKE?

The Bible tells us in many places that children will become like many things: (1) what they are around; (2) their teachers; and (3) what they are taught.

A Person Will Be Like Those Whom He Is Around

Both the Bible and practical experience tell us that a person becomes like those he is around. This is a well-known fact, evidenced by the response of parents when their child gets into trouble: "He started running with the wrong crowd." Of course, the Bible concurs with this when it says that bad morals corrupt good character: "Do not be deceived: 'Bad company ruins good morals'" 1 Corinthians 15:33 (RSV).[4]

However, we can use this to our advantage as parents. We need to become our children's primary influencers (with them spending more of their time with us than with peers). We must yield our lives to God in such a way that our training and example are models to follow. Then we can say the inverse of this passage in our children's lives: *Good morals, through parental involvement and modeling, create good character.*

A Student Will Be Like His Teacher

Luke 6:40 tells us that a student becomes like the one who teaches him: "A disciple is not above his teacher, but everyone who is perfectly trained will be like his teacher" Luke 6:40 (NKJV).[5] We hear this expressed over and over again in our society: "the apple doesn't fall far from the tree"; "they're out of the same mold"; "like father like son"; and more. Our children have a good chance of being just like us. Isn't that scary?

We had a recent experience in which Luke 6:40 was born out. Several years ago a friend of mine, I'll call Sue, had a sick mother-in-law who was about to die. I did not know where Sue's mother-in-law stood spiritually, so I felt led to visit her in the hospital in order to talk to her about her soul. Cami happened to be with me the day I was running errands, and we stopped in. Thankfully, after talking with this lady, I felt confident that she was not just a "church member" but was truly born again. On the way home, Cami and I talked extensively, as was our family's custom anytime one child was in the vehicle alone with me or Ray.

Many years later, when Cami was a senior in high school, Ray's great aunt from a few hours away was extremely sick and looked to be nearing the end of her life. She and Cami had become pen pals over the previous few years, and while this aunt often wrote to her about church activities, Cami did not feel confident about her salvation. So, she wrote this lady a long letter detailing salvation and how to be born again. Shortly thereafter, Cami heard back from Ray's great aunt saying that she had indeed been born again when she was a young girl and felt secure in her eternal destiny.

The girls are extensively involved in multiple aspects of ministry, so the fact that Cami checked on this aunt's spiritual condition did not surprise me. What surprised me was what she said several weeks ago as she and I drove by the hospital that my friend's mother-in-law had been in. Cami reminded me of when she was a little girl and had gone with me to talk to and pray with that lady. Then she said, "Did you know that's why I wrote to Aunt Betty about her salvation? I remembered going there with you and how you told me that if there is any question about someone's salvation, we have to find out before that person dies. I knew that I had to do the same thing for Aunt Betty that you had done for Sue's mother-in-law."

Truly, our children have the potential to be just like us, their teachers. They will take on many of our character qualities, acquire many of our talents, even make the same facial expressions, at times.

The transparency required and the expectations on us as parents, in order to help our children know and love God, are vast. It feels like such a heavy burden, and even unfair at times. But it is what we are called to. It is worrisome, and overwhelming, and such an incredible, awesome responsibility--all at the same time. We are called to raise and train our children in God's wisdom and truth; gaining and keeping their hearts is one way that we can do that.

SACRIFICES

Sacrificing for the Well-Trained Heart

As homeschoolers, we often feel like we have sacrificed so much for our children already: day in and day out spent with them, when the easier course would be to have someone else tend to them all day long; lack of income during the hours that we have chosen to train our children rather than work or pursue a career; with that lack of income, we often have less "things"--the remodeled kitchen, the larger house, the nicer car, etc.

Yet we have found that those sacrifices are often not enough. Depending on the number of children you have, the work hours of the father, the ages of the children, and so on, you may be called to even more than the "typical" homeschooling sacrifice.

Over fifteen years ago, when we had six children ten and under, we discovered that we were going to need make many sacrifices to raise our children in the well-trained heart way. We found that if we wanted to truly protect our children from negative influences, provide substitutions for those things that we were "removing" from their lives, and develop intimate communication with them, we were going to need to give most of my time and a great deal of Ray's time. In order to teach them the things we wanted them to know (academics, Bible, character, virtue of work, conflict resolution, relational training, and much more), the sacrifice of time would be substantial.

For many years, Ray was in the automotive industry, first as controller, then as materials manager, division controller, and eventually, plant manager. He worked a minimum of sixty hours a week from the time we were married until he left that line of work. We knew what we wanted to do in our children's lives, and we knew it could not be done unless we put all the time we could into them. So, Ray did almost nothing but work and spend time with the family--teaching early in the mornings before he went to work, leading us in worship and biblical studies around a late evening dinner table, and getting into the children's hearts as he put them to bed. His job took enough time so that any other activities were unthinkable--if we wanted to do what we knew was required in the heart training of our children.

From the time our oldest was eight or so until nearly ten years later, the majority of my time was spent at home, training the children, homeschooling, and everything related to those two. I wrote a little, encouraged homeschoolers informally as much as possible, did some hospitality, and that was it for "extras." For ten years, I never went to a sales party, seldom went shopping, had few friendships (which in hindsight was not the best thing), and stayed home most of the time. (It should be noted that if Ray's job had not been so demanding, and he had more time available to be with the children, I perhaps could have had more "outside activities." This was simply the way it was for us at the time.)

Now I am not mandating a martyr existence for all homeschoolers who want children with well-trained hearts, but there may be a season during your heart training when all else gets put on hold in order to carry out the callings of your parenting and child training. And the sacrifice may seem unreasonable and impossible. But we kept reminding ourselves that this was a season--a short season, really. And we also kept asking ourselves, *What else did we want to do in this world besides pass on the faith to our children?* We felt that we had a roadmap that would help us truly develop generational evangelism--and no sacrifice was too great for that calling.

Sacrifice of Fathers

In our conservative Christian sub-culture, it is noteworthy for a mother to sacrifice for her family, but a father is expected to do so on a much smaller scale. The whole idea of the husband's main job being breadwinner is so emphasized that his other responsibilities are often diminished. Not that working forty to sixty hours a week is not difficult. We know it is. But work should not be our life.

Yes, the Bible does say that if a man does not provide for his family, he is worse than an unbeliever.[6] But this is one calling on a man's life. There are many other callings that are overlooked or de-emphasized as a result of focusing on career. Also, there is a difference between climbing the corporate ladder, achieving success in the workplace, having a large income--and working to support one's family.

We appeal to you to consider this: If a man's providing for his family keeps him from his other equally important duties at home--

heart training, loving his wife as Christ loved the church, keeping his children from the world until they are more mature, leading his family, etc.--then maybe that avenue of providing for his family is too extensive, the price too high.

We discovered this in our lives, and we encourage each home-schooling dad to evaluate his entire life, job, hobbies, church work, service to others, sports, extended family, and more in order to see what the proper place of each should be during the season of life that he is in.

When Joshua and Kayla entered the teen years (the time debate came into our lives), we felt that it would be nearly impossible for us to raise teens the way we wanted to with Ray working sixty-plus hours a week. By that time, he was a plant manager in the automotive industry, and sixty hours was an easy week. He still poured himself into us when he came home and did early morning teaching with the children as he could, but the hours were just not enough to raise our teenagers the way we felt we should. However, we did not see that there was anything we could do about it. A high mortgage and a comfortable lifestyle seemed impossible to leave.

Then we had a jolting awakening--our eighth baby, Carly Grace, died in the womb during an intrauterine blood transfusion. I labored at the hospital for what was predicted to be three or four days due to my previous c-sections. (The doctor felt that I could endure the labor since Carly weighed just under a pound.) To make a long and painful story short, my uterus ruptured, and for several hours in the night, I was in life and death situations due to hemorrhaging, followed by a lengthy surgery resulting in the loss of my fertility.

Shortly after that, we sold our 4,000-plus square foot home (including a large, spacious basement) and moved into a 1,400 square foot home. We sold or gave away half of everything we owned, and Ray took a less demanding job from eight to five, weekdays only.

This was a huge sacrifice for all of us--for me and the kids as we got used to clothing from thrift stores almost exclusively and little space; for Ray as he gave up the challenges of running an entire plant for simply managing a small department at a non-automotive (non-high-paced) plant. However, we knew it was a sacrifice that we had to make in order to train our children the way we desired.

Financial Sacrifices

We gave up nearly forty percent of our income, a large house, a company car, and much more in the way of material sacrifices. We also had little money to buy and do those extra things that we were used to doing. Then we had other choices to make: new furniture or a weekend trip to Chicago museums? A nicer van or quality school books and tools? New pictures for the wall or a family night at the bowling alley with pizza afterward? And again, we had to make the hard choices: *things* would be available later; our children are only with us for a short time. We have not regretted those decisions (though I am greatly anticipating the day we have a comfortable and attractive sofa!).

Family or Ministry?

We feel that ministry outside the home and inside the home can co-exist, and should actually complement each other. However, either home (the physical aspect of creating and maintaining a home or the character and spiritual training of those within the home) or ministry can become too consuming and negate the other altogether.

Usually it is the home that suffers, not the outside ministry. Oftentimes, it seems that Christians can get so caught up in ministering to those outside their families that the ministry within their families gets overlooked. How many people do you know who dedicate inordinate amounts of time to preaching or teaching the gospel, helping the poor, or building up the body while shirking their responsibilities to train their own children in God's Word?

Just like hobbies and other outside activities, there is a time and season for everything. If a ministry keeps you from fulfilling your first calling of converting and discipling your own family members, it could be that you are operating outside of your current season.

The Bible indicates that when one fulfills his responsibilities inside his home, he is qualified to serve outside his home: "He must manage his own family well and see that his children obey him with proper respect" I Timothy 3:4 (NIV).[7] It is not "taking away from your ministry" to serve and train your family. It is "qualifying" you to be in ministry.

MARRIAGE AND THE WTH

Marriage Is the Training Grounds for Beginning the Well-Trained Heart Approach

Marriage is the training grounds for living for God in so many areas. When two people marry, they are forced to learn to display the character of Christ and live together contentedly, or each one lives for himself or herself and they live together unhappily. Through the daily ins and outs of marriage, and eventually, through living with our children, we learn how to yield, yield, yield--the key to living for Christ.

You see it's easy to get along with others whom we are not always with. It is not difficult to be friendly to those you do not have to deal with day in and day out. But it is another story to live a Christ-focused life with someone who drives you crazy at times! As we display proper attitudes and behaviors toward our spouse, our children see that it is possible to live this Christian life at home. They see the model for how they should treat their siblings--and eventually their own spouses.

There is a common adage that the way a boy treats his mother is the same way he will treat his wife. However, shortly after our son's wedding in 2004, he related that he did not feel that this saying was accurate. His perception was that however a boy treats his sister will reveal how he will treat his wife since the brother-sister relationship is more lateral while the mother-son relationship is more hierarchical.

Siblings need mutual submission in order to get along in much the same way that husbands and wives do. Children learn how to treat siblings by seeing how their parents treat each other, and this eventually carries over into their own marriages. Yes, all family relationships are training grounds for future relationships.

Modeling Godly Relationships in Marriage

We do not have the space in this book to elaborate on many marriage issues, but we have found that the depth of our love and respect for each other is mirrored in our children's love and respect for us and each other. In our marriage, we have come to understand and appreciate the husband-wife roles outlined in Ephesians. However, we see an unbalance in conservative Christian circles that we feel takes the focus in marriage off of mutual submission and deference to each other and on to husband and wife roles too much.

We believe that children would learn more about living godly character and selflessness in marriage if Christians focused more on the love, mutual submission, and constant service to each other that the Bible teaches rather than simply teaching who should be doing what via roles. Our children have respected us for this. They have seen other marriages in which the wife is unhappy or the husband wields too much power and not enough kindness and servanthood. They have a much healthier view of marriage, and a more biblically accurate one, we think, than children from families whose marriage teaching centers predominately around Ephesians 5:22 [8] while not applying other verses to the marriage relationship, such as Ephesians 5:21, [9] I Corinthians 13, [10] the one anothers that Jesus taught,[11] and other lifestyle and character instruction of the Bible.

Yes, our children understand the biblical concept of husband and wife roles. They understand that the husband is the head of the family, and the wife ultimately must submit to his leading. However, and more importantly, they know---and have witnessed their entire lives---that when a husband and wife love and serve one another with no regard for who "the boss" is and no regard for one's own power and "rights," a marriage can be a truly "Christian" marriage.

House Divided Against Itself Shall Not Stand

One parenting concept that we were taught early on in our marriage is that of Matthew 12:25: "...a house divided against itself shall not stand."[12] We were instructed that as applied to marriage, this verse indicates that we will not stand as a married couple or as a family if we are divided.

Of course, Scripture teaches that when a couple is united in marriage, they are to become one. Whole books are written about the implications of this---physical oneness, spiritual oneness, etc. But for our purposes here as homeschooling parents, the combined advice to become one (unified) and to not be divided from within demonstrates to us the importance of unity in our marriage. We must do all that we can as husbands and wives to protect the unity of our marriage. This unity spills over extensively into the unity of our entire family.

What God Has Joined Together

Jesus made it clear that when we marry, we become one---and that nothing should alter than oneness: "So they are no longer two, but one. Therefore what God has joined together, let man not separate" Matthew 19:6 (NIV).[13]

We often focus on the fact that we have to protect our marriages from outsiders trying to destroy them. However, we have seen many marriages that are not hurt by outside influences, but instead by inside influences: the children.

While we believe wholly in sacrificing for our children, we do not believe in sacrificing the marriage relationship. This "marriage sacrifice" often happens in families with spoiled, selfish children who are coddled and indulged by a mother who simply cannot say no to them, even at the expense of her marriage relationship. It sometimes happens when we allow the busy-ness of too many activities for our children steal away time that is needed to remain intimate with our mate. Sometimes it is the father who puts the children ahead of his relationship with his wife. He may allow the children's wants and wishes to come before the needs of the marriage.

Again, it seems to us that there is a hierarchy in Scripture. Man and wife were created and joined as one first. Then came children. Even in a practical sense, we would probably all agree that we are better, stronger, more loving, and saner parents when our marriage is healthy.

No One Can Serve Two Masters

Another parenting concept associated with marriage that we were introduced to early is that of serving two masters. In talking to the rich young ruler about his salvation, Jesus said that serving both money and God was incompatible. It was not possible to be mastered by money (greed) and mastered by God: "No one can serve two masters; for either he will hate the one and love the other, or else he will be loyal to the one and despise the other. You cannot serve God and mammon" Matthew 6:24 (NKJV).[14]

The same thing is true in our families. Our children cannot serve two (un-unified) masters. We must be unified in our marriage, and our children must (1) know that we are unified; and (2) not be allowed to cause disunity in it.

A child is serving two masters when he comes to one parent with a request and gets an answer he is not happy with, then turns to the other parent in hopes of getting a satisfactory answer. He is serving two masters--he knows which buttons to push on each parent, and he is dividing his parents as he does so.

This verse continues, saying that if you try to serve two masters, you will love one and hate the other or cling to one and despise the other. We can all point to families in which this application is played out: a child clings to the parent who gives him his own way, and despises the parent who is "harder," who does not give in to the child. When we are not unified, we force our child to choose one master--and often to despise the one he does not choose.

Recognizing this, we made a firm rule early in our parenting that our child absolutely could not come to one of us with a request, get a negative response, then go to the other with the same request. When we do this, we are forcing him to serve two masters--and choose the one who will give him the answer he wants.

Now there have been times when one of the children went to Ray or me about the other parent, asking us to talk to the other about some misunderstanding or lack of discernment the one parent may be displaying. But even then, we do not say that the other parent is wrong, simply that we will talk about it and try to get it solved. Sometimes it may be a misunderstanding or unclear communication that can be clarified with the additional perspective of another person. Hopefully, the offending parent will admit his or her guilt in the situation, but it is divisive for the non-offending parent to talk about the other parent's guilt behind his or her back.

IT STARTS IN OUR HEARTS

Getting and keeping our children's hearts, then helping them to learn to live lives that glorify God and are of service to others, can only happen when we have those things in our hearts first. This was revealed to me over a dozen years ago when my kids were acting just like me! I soon understood that my children would never be anything that I was not. In marriage, in our level of contentment, in our behavior towards our children, in our outside ministries--in everything--our children will seldom be what we are not willing or able to be ourselves. The poem below came out of that experience.

I Looked Into the Eyes of My Children

I looked into the eyes of my children, surprised by what I
did see,
For I thought I'd see the face of Jesus, staring back at me.
But then when I observed their hearts, what I saw was a
big surprise.
For instead, I saw me--their mother--reflected in their
eyes.
All that I wish I wasn't, all that I would like to change,
Was displayed right there in their eyes, in many different
ways.
All the things I wanted them to change, all the things I dis-
liked the most,
Were merely reflections of me--things I should have
already known.
I cried to the Lord, "Forgive me, for pressuring them, you see,
To be things that I am not willing, or even able-to be."

When I heard an older one say, in such a selfish tone,
"I'll give you my best toy, if you'll just leave me alone."
I saw manipulation take place and knew where it was learned,
For I, too, can be the very same way, the conniving way I
spurned.
When I saw one of them wanting the best, I thought, "What
a selfish child,"
Then I saw myself being selfish in just a little while.
When I heard one of them talk angrily, I couldn't believe my
ears,
Until a few minutes later, my own angry voice did I hear.
I saw one of them putting frivolities before the things of the
Lord,
And then I saw me with my magazines, instead of God's
holy Word.

Day after day, God showed me, my children learn what they live,
And before I can help them to change, I must be willing to give-
Yes, give up the things that keep me-- from being what God wants me to be-
And be willing to be an example, of Jesus for my children to see.
Now when I find negative character reflected in my children's eyes,
I look into the mirror, for it's no longer such a surprise.
Instead of asking them to change, I ask God to work in me,
And day by day, changes in them take place---and Christ I am able to see. [15]

"Let It Begin With Me"
Discussion/Application Questions
-- Chapter 5 --

1. Do you agree that mothers set the tone for the family? Does your family feel like you are unhappy or difficult if things are not going your way? How can you begin to show contentment regardless of circumstances?
2. If you have trouble being close and intimate to family members, how do you feel about the idea that you should try to change that aspect of yourself? Do you think the verses about our relationships as husbands and wives and parents indicate that we cannot make excuses for those things?
3. Can you think of positive character qualities or habits that your children have that are direct reflections of you? How about negative ones?
4. Think back to a time that you corrected your child for something that you yourself do or that you are like. How could you have responded differently to change that within yourself?
5. Is God calling you to sacrifice even more for the training of your children? What are these sacrifices? What are the steps you will take to make them?
6. Fathers, in evaluating your career, hobbies, free time activities, church responsibilities, etc., is too much of your time consumed with less important things than the training of your children?
7. Do you need to make some changes in finances? Do you spend money on temporal things more than you do in investing in your children--family times, training materials, etc.?
8. Fathers, how can you begin turning your hearts more toward your children, so that they, in turn, will turn their hearts toward you?
9. Does your marriage have a loving, one-another focus, or do you focus on roles so much that you lose the heart of the biblical teaching?

SIX

First Things First

Prioritizing and the Well-Trained Heart

Priorities Are What You Do

Probably the greatest hindrance to getting anything done in life is that of misplaced priorities. That is especially true in the case of family living and heart training of our children since those are often non-measurable, non-visual pursuits.

Everyone has priorities. Some have their priorities listed and checked off daily or weekly. Some prioritize by default. Their priorities are not planned, but they have priorities nonetheless--since priorities are what a person does.

If you were to pull out your daytimer, family calendar, or daily to-do lists, anyone could read them and give you a list of your priorities. You might argue about their observations. You might say, "No, that thing is not my priority. My priority is this..." Something loftier, more noble, or more similar to what you would like your priorities to be. However, if you do not do something consistently, it is not a priority; it is simply a wish. *Because prioritities are what you do.*

The same concept is revealed with your checkbook. You can say that certain things are the most important to you, but when you open your checkbook, the dearest things to you are revealed.

Check Out Your Calendar

An eye-opening exercise for anyone is to evaluate--hour by hour, day by day--what you have done over the past month. How much time did you devote to corporate worship, God's Word, knowing Christ, prayer, praise, ministry, and discipleship? How much time did you watch television, play sports, surf the web, or read a novel? How much time did you spend with your spouse? How much time did you devote to training your children? Break these activities down to determine how much of each waking day you spent on each one. The activities that you spent the greatest amount of time on are your priorities. If you watched television and movies for twelve hours this week and spent three hours discipling your young adults, then your priority is entertainment--not training (at least for that week).

From my list of activities, I can tell what my true priorities are. I might think my priorities are God; my husband; my children; homeschooling; saving time; being organized; my extended family; keeping my children involved in meaningful activities (those that teach them to become organized, study, love learning, develop their own priorities, and be close to the Lord); building relationships; releasing of our teens and young adults slowly while discipling and mentoring them; and family ministries. However, if my calendar does not show the majority of my time being used in those pursuits, then they are not my priorities. They are simply my wishes--my hopes and dreams of what I want to do, but not what I actually do.

Yes to Something; No to Something Else

One of the great truths in time management--one that Ray and I have continually reminded ourselves of--is that when you say yes to something, you say no to something else. There is not enough time for everything. So, in saying yes to something, you are using up some of the limited amount of time that you have. You are filling a time slot with that activity, instead of some other activity. So, you are saying yes to one thing in that time slot--and no to something else that could go in that same time slot. Seldom does a person feel that he or she has time for everything; thus, *when we say yes to one thing, we are saying no to something else.*

Now, obviously, we could get all hung up on this and never do anything relaxing because that recreational activity is replacing something more noble or more productive. We could become so consumed with doing and accomplishing that we squeeze other people out of our lives. That is not desired either. Time with others, relaxation, and fun are all important aspects of our lives, too.

However, a thorough understanding of the fact that time is consumable--there is only so much of it--is necessary. It is so much harder to say no to outsiders (to say no to coaching baseball, leading speech and debate, working on a Christmas play, etc.) than it is to say no to those who are closest to us. If we learn to prioritize well, we can say yes to those things that we have determined ahead of time are priorities and no to those things that are not current priorities.

PRIORITY PURGING

The List

We learned about prioritizing early in our marriage, and I am forever grateful that we did. Twenty-three years ago, Ray and I (at ages twenty-four and twenty) had a two year old little boy. We were active in our church and with our extended families. We wanted to "do it all" for the Lord and for others. However, we found ourselves, even with only one child and at our young ages, so busy that we could not keep up.

One evening we sat down with the calendar and wrote on it everything we felt that we should do or participate in during that month: men's Bible study, ladies' Bible study, Ray's extended family, my extended family, Ray's master's degree, church three times a week, home care groups, hospitality, family night, nursing home visitation, church outreach, etc.

This full calendar page has become known to us through the years as "the list." When we were finished, we discovered that if we did everything we thought we should do, everything we wanted to do, and everything we had to do, we would need sixty evenings that month!

Life was controlling us, rather than us controlling life. How many of us feel this way today, especially among homeschoolers, who tend to be over-achievers, over-do-ers, and over-extenders anyway? We find ourselves doing things that are not really our priorities (or things that we do not desire as our priorities) and not doing the things that we really want as our priorities.

This is not a new concept. Paul said this very thing in the Bible: "I do not understand my own actions. For I do not do what I want, but I do the very thing I hate" (Romans 7:15 RSV).[1] This is an age-old problem that even one of Christ's strongest early followers felt.

At that point, we decided that something had to go. We obviously did not have sixty evenings a month to do that list. We decided to take action. We had our first "priority purge."

Prioritizing Takes Action

Prioritizing takes action! It is something you do--or else it is done for you. Ray and I had to take good things off of our calendar in order to make room for the best things. We had to say no to average things in order to say yes to excellent things.

That is another important concept in prioritizing: each person's priorities are his own. We do not need to have identical priorities to our friends. We do not need to do everything someone else does. Our priorities are personal; they are the God-ordained objectives in our own lives for that time period.

If you want to have solid, Christ-honoring priorities, you must take action. You must determine, with your spouse and with God's guidance, what your priorities are. This is the tricky part; everything seems important. Everything is crying out for attention and help. How do we know what should be priorities in our lives? How do we know what to spend our time on?

DETERMINING PRIORITIES

Prioritize With Your Spouse

Hopefully, you and your spouse have the same goals in life. If that is the case, then you both want the same things: to live lives that please and honor God; to have godly, well educated children; to make a difference in the world; etc. But there are so many ways to please and honor God; there are so many ways to educate our children (even within the homeschool arena); there are so many ways to make a difference in the world.

If you and your spouse are on the same page with your priorities, I recommend that you go through the rest of this chapter about determining priorities together. Talking through your goals, dreams, and visions together will help to further solidify your priorities--and what you should be spending your life on.

Prioritize Based on Boundaries Already in Place in Your Life: People and Situations

Many things that should be our priorities are staring us right in the face, literally. God has already placed people in our lives that are built in priorities. They are already there--they just need to be prioritized.

For example, if you have children, a husband, and a call to homeschool, these are boundaries--built-in priorities--that should take precedence over other things. They are placed in your life by God Himself. He is giving you ready-made priorities and is just waiting for you to put them high on your priority list where they belong.

More Boundaries: Talents and Skills

Another built-in boundary that aids in prioritizing is that of talents and skills. As we recognize talents and skills that God has given us, we can safely assume that God wants those as priorities in our lives--or wants to use them to help us reach those priorities.

For example, if you are a gifted musician, more than likely God wants you to use that talent in your life. It will quite possibly play a role in developing your priorities during each phase of your life. Combine this with the first built-in priority--the people in your life--and you can further see how this talent might be used of God in determining and fulfilling your priorities. If you have small children, but God has impressed upon you (the wife) to help bring in income for your family (and you and your husband determine that that is a priority), maybe giving music lessons will help you achieve your priority of developing more income. In this way you are using your talents and still maintaining your built-in priority of homeschooling and taking care of small children.

Your skills and talents were given especially to you. When my older children were younger, I always wanted to do and be something other than what I was. I especially envied other people's talents. For instance, I saw musical families and wished that we could be musical. I wanted all of us to be up on stage somewhere playing instruments together. However, I was not given the skills of music, nor were Ray and many of the children.

Using the skills that I have, rather than wanting others' skills, saves time and gives me more energy to meet the priorities God has given me. We have chosen to focus on the skills that God has given our family: some are intellectually gifted; most of us are organizers; we are all communicators (in writing and speech); we are all leaders. By focusing on those skills, rather than skills that we do not have, we can meet our priorities more efficiently and more excellently.

Still More Boundaries: Seasons of Life

Our next "priority purge" came a few years later when we had two small children. God led us to attend two awesome, life-changing seminars: The Christian Homeschooling Workshop[2] and the Advanced Homeschooling Workshop[3] by Gregg Harris. From these seminars, among many other things, we learned about seasons of life.

A season of life is that time period you find yourself in based on your age, your family situation, etc. We discovered that we were not being as effective as we could be in our lives because we were trying to do things out of our season.

At that time, according to the workshop, we were in the "Business and Babies" season. We stayed there for many, many years! Yet, we continually found ourselves involved in activities that were for those of the next season. Ray was on the hospital board in our town, he was an elder in our church, we taught Bible classes at church to people three times our age. We struggled to find time to attend meetings, serve in the church thoroughly, prepare our lessons, etc., due to Ray's heavy work schedule and our responsibilities with our young children.

We came home from those two seminars and went through another priority purging. Due to the season that we were in, we decided Ray should resign from his hospital board and elder positions. We also cut back on our teaching at church. After all, we were still in our early twenties. What business did we have telling others how to live their lives when we lacked the wisdom that we would obtain through years of experiences? Another priority purge helped us get closer to our God-given priorities for that season.

So, not only do we have built-in priorities because we have children to homeschool and a spouse to love and encourage, but the ages of those children and spouse further solidify our priorities, usually also based on the season of life we are in. When I had five children ten and under, I loved homeschooling and communicating so much that I wanted to write and speak about homeschooling. I saw others doing it, read others' books, etc, and I felt that I had a lot to offer homeschoolers since I had been a teacher, had been homeschooling for several years, and had, had many experiences helping homeschoolers get started. However, learning about seasons of life helped me to see that it was not time for those things. Maybe I did have some built-in boundaries of skills (speaking, writing, and communicating). Maybe I did have the motivation due to my love for homeschooling. However, the other built-in boundaries of so many young children, my season of life, the lack of experience for myself, etc., showed me that it was not the right time for that priority of communicating with larger groups of homeschoolers extensively.

More Boundaries Again: Natural Seasons

And taking the whole built-in boundaries concept one step further, we find that even natural seasons of life (winter, spring, summer, and fall)--when combined with the built-in priorities of people, talents, and life seasons--help us determine our priorities.

Priorities and schedules are fluid, not stagnant. They change constantly, especially when we have young children and we are homeschooling. For example, in the fall, we might have a newborn baby who nurses and sleeps, giving us a lot of time to school the kids, do the housework, minister to other women, etc. However, two natural seasons later, in the spring, that same sleeping infant is a curious, crawling toddler, altering our schedule and, in effect, our priorities! Suddenly, we do not have the long hours to read around the table with everyone in attendance. If we still have the priority of reading together, we may have to limit it, prioritize the training of that toddler, or read in groups so someone is available to look after the little tyke. A natural season of life affects our priorities, and we have to decide how to handle it, what our priority will be for that season, etc.

Each year, new priorities pop up. Maybe you haven't had a new reader for three years, and now your "caboose" needs daily reading instruction, time that had formally been given to other things. A natural season (i.e. a child in first or second grade) influences your prioritizing. Yes, new priorities will emerge, but the decision to make something a priority and delete something else should be a conscious decision, not a decision that is made for you by outside forces.

ADDING AND REMOVING

When You Add Something to Your Life, Remove Something Else

This brings us to another important prioritizing truth: when you add something to your life, you need to remove something else to make room for the new thing. Just about everyone is maxed out. We are nearly all living on the edge. So, how can we add anything else into an already busy life? The only way we can do this is to remove something that is presently there.

First Things First

In the case of the "toddling toddler" described above, if we are adding into our schedules the extra time and attention that little one requires, we need to remove something else (i.e. part of our read aloud time?) in order to accommodate another addition to the day. In the case of the new reader, you will need to remove something that takes thirty minutes a day from your life in order to add the extra reading lessons to your day.

This is especially important for new homeschoolers. When I talk to new homeschooling moms, I often ask them if they were busy prior to their homeschooling. They always answer yes, and list myriad things they were previously doing. Then I drop the bomb: *What are you going to remove from your schedule in order to have the four to eight hours a day (depending on the number of children she will be schooling and the ages of those children, as well as the curriculum she is using)* to homeschool? You cannot do the same things you used to do if you are adding four to eight hours a day to your schedule!

We use this concept with space in our home as well. We have a small house, only fourteen hundred square feet. Before Joshua got married, we had four boys in one bedroom and three girls in another, and Mom and Dad's room tripled as a library and pantry. We have an ongoing rule that nobody can bring anything into the house unless he takes something out. If the girls have a good day at thrift stores, they are to come in and remove the number of clothing items they just purchased. There simply is no space for anything else. Something has to go. The same is true of time.

Eternal Value

We have said that each person's priorities are his own and will be different; however, as Christians, we are all called to love our neighbors as ourselves and make disciples. Our priorities should reflect things of eternal value.

This is where it gets even stickier. What is too much emphasis on temporal things and not enough on eternal? How do we lead our children into learning the value of spending time on God's kingdom rather than the kingdom here on earth?

Nobody can determine those things for you but you. However, we challenge you to take the infamous "end of lifetime test." If you were on your deathbed, would you wish you had been in more clubs and activities or would you wish you had discipled your children more? Would you wish you had made more money or made more disciples?

In the well-trained heart area, would you wish that you had put your son in three sports a year or memorized three chapters of Scripture a year with him? Would you wish that you had driven around four days a week from three to seven for kids' activities or would you wish you had spent four afternoons a week getting into your children's hearts?

It is true. You alone can determine your priorities. But without placing eternal value on them, they might be the wrong priorities for you and your family. They might not truly be what God is calling you to.

PUTTING IT ALL TOGETHER

Narrowing Down "The List"

Back to our original priority purging: we had to narrow down the list. The sixty activities would not fit into thirty evenings. So, we listed our priorities--those things that we truly felt that God desired for our life at that time. We recognized that we had built-in boundaries (a young son that I was home with all day, a demanding job for Ray that consumed at least sixty hours a week, etc.). Then we determined what we believed God would have us do with the small amount of time we had remaining.

This list was fairly general at that time: Ray's job, Joshua, our extended family, growing in the Lord, hospitality, etc. From that list of "priorities," we looked at our sixty-night-to-do-list and decided what activities on that list would help us meet our priorities. We didn't know a lot about seasons of life and prioritizing at that time, but we did the best we could. It was a step in the process of establishing mature priorities.

We decided that in order to meet our priorities, we had to get rid of the good things on our list and keep the best things. We had to eliminate the average things and retain the excellent things. We had to spend our time on those things that would help us meet our priorities.

Saying No

From your priority list, you can discern what you should say yes to and what you should say no to. If you have your eight, ten, or twelve priorities listed based on the built-in boundaries of your life, then you can examine each activity and opportunity based on whether it helps you meet your priorities or not.

For example, if I were asked to teach a Sunday school class, I would have to say that I could not do it now. At the time of this writing, we are busy getting our ministry and publishing company off the ground. Since it would hinder me from achieving the priorities I know I am supposed to do right now, I would decline that offer for the time being.

The same thing is true, for instance, of a homeschooling mom who is also a pastor's wife. If she were asked to lead a homeschooling event, she might have to say no, since she is already tied up with the duties of her built-in priority of being a pastor's wife, with church activities and responsibilities.

What About Volunteering?

Sometimes when people hear us talk about dropping good and keeping the best, they say, "If everyone did that, then nobody would be available to teach Sunday school, help the elderly, or mow the church lawn." However, we think the opposite would happen if our advice were followed.

If everyone were doing things based on his or her built-in boundaries of family, talents, seasons of life, and natural seasons, all work for God everywhere would get done. Those with young children would spend the majority of their time generating income to meet family needs and tending to the little ones; those with more time would do the areas they were called to; the little ones would grow up being well-trained and take their places in the circle of priorities--and even more could be done for the Lord.

Be Consistent and Gracious

People are often threatened by people who know what they want in life and go for it. Those ambitious people seem so confident and goal-oriented that it is sometimes offensive to those who feel as though they are floundering. Add to that the fact that homeschoolers are often scrutinized, and sometimes legitimately so. For those reasons, we can't stress enough the importance of being consistent in your prioritizing (not picking and choosing what you will do on a whim) and being gracious in your interactions with others.

We hurt others and God's work when we look down on those who do not have the same priorities as we do, or when we minimize someone else's goals and priorities and act as though ours are superior to theirs. Consistency and graciousness are the rules of order for maintaining priorities in front of others.

If you are truly a prioritized person doing what God wants you to do, you will have to say no to things, but our no should not be one that denotes that we have better things to do that what was asked of us. It should not be a "no" that elevates our goals and activities above others. If you truly are unable to serve in that capacity, graciously say that you are unable to take on the task at hand, then be about what you should be about!

However, there are many tasks and activities that can be done even by the busiest people, especially when you work together as a family. We have found that we can do things for others that we didn't think we had time for when we do these things together. For example, we often all cook together to make meals or treats for people or special occasions. When we used to host debate and speech tournaments, we found that we could relieve other parents' stress and extra hours by all working together here at home to prepare ballot packets, make food for judges, figure pairings, etc. It is amazing what several people, intent on serving others, can accomplish when they work together.

MORE PRIORITY PURGING

I have already described a couple of the priority purges we have experienced in our lives. There have been several more of these over the years. I can't emphasize enough the importance of paying attention to the priority purging that might naturally happen in your life. These purges may very well be God's way of steering you in a certain direction in terms of your priorities.

The Move

Many years ago, when we had five children ten and under, Ray's plant shut down, and he was transferred to another plant in a city an hour away from our hometown. We had always lived in the same area as our parents, the community in which we were born and went to school. Moving with five young children to a community where we did not know anyone was overwhelming at first, but proved to be God's way of purging our priorities even further.

Our move took us away from the church we had been in since our early married years, away from our families, and away from our friends. However, God used it to help us focus on the most important priority we had: our children. We didn't know anyone in our new town. We didn't have a church. We didn't have extended family just up the road to go play games with or visit. We didn't have any outside activities. It was just us--our marriage, five young children, homeschooling, and Ray's job.

Talk about priority purging! This move forced us to bind together in our marriage and with our children more than ever. We were not distracted by outside friendships for us or the children--and our family unity, child training, and marriage were all strengthened as a result of it. We could have used this time to dig into even more busy-ness and activity or rush to find new friends, but because we took this as God's way of making us more strongly united, and we focused on the heart-training of our children rather than outside things, this priority purge became a turning point in our family's life. New friends and activities would come later, after the priority of strengthening our family was well underway.

Job Change

I have already mentioned the loss of our eighth baby in utero and Ray's job change, but the two are actually quite linked and provided even more priority purging in our lives. In 1999, we had seven children, ages fifteen down to one. Ray's job as a plant manager in an automotive plant was becoming more and more unbearable as he worked sixty to seventy hours a week to keep everything running smoothly. Joshua and Kayla were fifteen and twelve years old and our simple, tidy schedule of Ray teaching the kids before work, doing devotions during a late night dinner, then spending little spurts of time with each child before bed was unraveling. It had worked okay for the previous fifteen years because I stayed home most of the time and picked up the slack--and the children were younger and were not as high need emotionally and spiritually. The few minutes before bed with Dad had been sufficient. Our Sundays together, and anytime we had at all, had been maximized and adequate.

However, we began to realize the needs of teens were drastically different than the needs of ten year olds and babies. They required much more time and energy in order to raise them the way we felt that God wanted us to. Basically, we wanted out of our demanding lifestyle, but felt helpless to do so with a high mortgage and comfortable lifestyle. How could Ray change jobs and take a pay cut with the bills and lifestyle we had acquired?

So we put it on the back burner--until the weekend our unborn baby died and my life was in jeopardy. When that weekend was over, everything looked different. We came out of that whole ordeal with even stronger, more narrowed priorities--God and family were all that mattered.

As mentioned before, we sold or gave away half of everything we owned, moved to a little, old country house, and had a new life. Ray went from working a minimum of sixty (but often up to eighty) hours a week to working a normal forty hour a week job. We had hours and hours each week to devote to our new priorities--reaching and keeping the hearts of our teens. We didn't have much money. We didn't have many things. But we had the greatest commodity of all: time. Again, an outside influence took us through a priority purge that we could either recognize and utilize for our family's benefit or not. Nothing happens by accident. Watch for and learn from the priority purges God brings into your life.

DEVELOPING PRIORITIES FOR OUR CHILDREN

Heart training cannot take place when we are not with our children! That sounds so obvious, yet many of us shuttle our children from one activity to another, forcing us to be apart a great deal of the time and causing the family to be separated too much. Then we wonder why we can't get and keep our children's hearts. They are busy giving them to other people and activities along the way.

Nobody can choose the activities that your family will participate in. You know your priorities; you know your built-in boundaries; you know the callings on your life and the lives of your children. However, there are several benchmarks that we have found for choosing activities for our children that we would like to share with you--to help you reduce some of the busy-ness of your lives and give you more time for the eternal things you are called to.

1. Can more than one of our children do it at the same time? This is an important benchmark for us with seven children. The more things they can do together, the more efficient the activity will be and the more time we will have to be all together than if they were each in different activities.

2. Is it something we cannot do better, more easily, less expensively, or just as well at home? If so, we do it at home (for us, this means elaborate youth activities, much Bible teaching for children, etc.). If not, we participate in it outside of our home. For example, we feel that it is better to do speech and debate in a group in order to critique each other and learn from each other; outside teachers in Spanish, voice, sewing, and piano have done for us what we could not do or would not have done nearly as well for the time allotment.

3. Is it an activity that builds your children's character or spiritual lives (that still cannot be done at home or is truly done in a superior way if we take part in it). For instance, Bible quizzing or girls' accountability club, etc.

4. Is it a lot of bang for our buck--timewise? Is it a significantly advantageous activity that is worth the time to get there (especially since we live thirty minutes or more from most of our kids' activities)? If we spend two hours round trip to get to a class that only ends up with fifteen minutes of Bible instruction due to the numbers and ages of the children; the chaos of large group instruction; short attention spans of some children, etc., is it worth it? How much better can that three hours be spent at home together?

5. For older kids only (twelve to fourteen and older), does it seem to have something to do with what God has for their futures (i.e. music, drama, speaking, signing, office skills, computer skills, photography, etc.)? Note: We have never been among those who felt that trying

dozens of things from ages six to twelve via outside activities is that beneficial. At those ages, children are generally too young to know if soccer will really be their futures, and it seldom is. (We might choose soccer for exercise and fellowship, but we are realistic enough not to put too much stock in it as an indicator of a child's future, and we do not participate in it with the intention of "preparing our child for his future.")

6. Is it an opportunity to serve that we cannot provide ourselves or that is provided in a unique way, such as a service opportunity that we truly think will benefit them and others (no twenty-four hour rock-a-thons, please!)?

7. Are there negative influences that would negate involvement in it, such as too much unstructured peer time, too much emphasis on self or winning, too much independence from parents and siblings too early, etc.)?

8. Does it line up with our priorities--those things that we have listed that are the most important things for our family? Does it help accomplish those priorities or does it detract from those priorities?

It is imperative that we actually sit down and make decisions concerning our priorities, rather than letting life make those decisions for us. It is so difficult to know what is best for us, much less our children. Many people feel that we only have our children for eighteen years, so we should give them as many opportunities and activities as possible. We, too, believe we only have our children for eighteen years--thus, we should spend as much time training their hearts as we can humanly spend. Activities and opportunities are often temporal and can come with high price tags of time, money, and peer influences, whereas heart training is eternal. We need to prioritize to achieve the eternal.

"First Things First"
Discussion/Application Questions
-- Chapter 6 --

1. Do the "calendar check" with your spouse and discuss how you have spent the last month of your life. Did you spend it on what you thought were your priorities?
2. Discuss the idea of saying yes to some things and no to others. What things have you said no to recently that you wish you had not? What things have you said yes to that forced you to say no to something else?
3. Do you feel that you are controlling your life or is life controlling you?
4. What built-in boundaries of people and situations are already in your life? How can you elevate these things to the priority status they deserve?
5. Do you find yourself desiring others' skills and talents rather than appreciating and utilizing your own? What skills and talents could you put to more use in your life and in serving God and others?
6. Do you feel that your are meeting the priorities that are in your life due to the "season of life" you are in--the ages of your children, the needs of your extended family, the stage of your marriage, etc.?
7. Is your life maxed out because you continually add to it without deleting something to make room for the additions? What things can you remove to live the life God wants you to live right now?
8. Do you feel that your priorities (the things you spend your time on) are of eternal value?
9. Have you offended people in your life by acting as though your life and callings are more important than theirs? If so, how can you make amends in those situations?
10. Do you have benchmarks and guidelines for choosing activities for your children or do you haphazardly sign them up for whatever sounds interesting?
11. Do you find that your children are involved in so many activities that you do not have the training time needed to help them prepare to serve God and others throughout their lives?
12. Are activities and things replacing heart training in your family?

SEVEN

Recipe for Rebellion

Rules and the Well-Trained Heart

Part I: Four Ingredients of the Recipe for Rebellion

Poor prioritizing and following what we call the "Recipe for Rebellion" are two of the most significant hindrances to homeschooling the well-trained heart way. Like the prioritizing problem, the Recipe for Rebellion also requires its own chapter--it is that much of a hindrance to living out the well-trained heart in our homes.

As indicated numerous places in this book, we have believed in giving our children the reasons for our requests and rules (as long as the children are not demanding them), mostly due to embracing Kevin Leman's writings,[1] which we discovered early in our parenting. However, we did not realize the importance of our rules and requests being logical and understandable to our kids until after we began debate. Thus, we have determined four key ingredients in a Recipe for Rebellion that we will elaborate on in the pages of this chapter.

Recipe for Rebellion
Rules Without Reasons
Rules Without Response
Rules Without Repetition
Rules Without Relationship

INGREDIENT #1: RULES WITHOUT REASONS

Through our experience with speech and debate, we learned that not only should we give our children the reasons for our rules if possible, but that those reasons should be logical, scriptural, and understandable. Thus, our debate training of evidence and logic became even more important.

Evidence and Logic

We started to see the importance of evidence and logic, but that is not to say that we became completely analytical. We believe the Christian faith is a uniquely intimate, relational faith--one filled with love, sacrifice, and devotion. However, studying the Bible should be a combination of relational thinking (understanding God's heart towards us) and analytical study.

As you will see throughout this chapter, any discussion of rules or lifestyle boundaries for our children includes logic and evidence, as well as relationship. We have purposely tried to train our more intellectual children to also be relational and our predominantly relational children to be more logical. A well-rounded, impacting Christian needs both aspects in his life.

Hermaneutics

Thankfully, when our children were younger, we had already taught them much about hermanuetics, the branch of theology that deals with the principles of biblical exegesis (understanding the Bible). We just didn't always apply it to our thinking of rules and guidelines for living. We had previously taught the children how to look up words in the original language; how to use a concordance, Bible dictionary, Bible handbook, and other Bible helps; the place of non-authority Bible-time books (Josephus, etc.); how to cross reference Bible verses to see what another author of a book in the Bible said about the same subject, etc. We also had them use many Bible study books and complete many Bible lessons throughout their school years. Remember, we learned early on that faith was first, then character, so those were already in place.

Now, I am not a heady person; we taught our children much about hermaneutics through our homeschool curriculum, various Bible study books, and creation seminars. Hermeneutics is not a subject one can discuss in a paragraph; there are volumes and volumes written about it, most of which are beyond my comprehension. However, in training our children's hearts well, we have found that rules without reasons can significantly alienate our children from us. This is especially true with our teens and young adults. For this reason, I have been learning the rudimentary basics of this subject in order to study what we believe and why we believe it with our children even more. This general understanding has helped us when we read books together, when we discuss topics, as well as when we encounter information apart from one another.

Applying Logic and Hermaneutics

I mentioned earlier how we began studying our rules and beliefs with our older children. In the beginning, we just used the Bible with concordances, Bible dictionaries, study Bibles (with cross-referencing applications), and Bible study computer programs at hand. However, as our teens have become young adults, we have also done book studies, article studies, and re-hashing of sermons and messages together. From these studies, we have learned--and have been able to teach our teens and young adults--to discern the meaning of written material, audio presentations, and video teaching more carefully.

A good example of this is in a book study that we did with our two oldest daughters during their recent summer off from college. We wanted to delve deeper into women's roles, especially pertaining to leadership in the church and working for God's kingdom outside of the home (as opposed to homemaking only). In an effort to get a broad range of ideas and opinions, we took two extreme books about the topic--one from a more “liberal,” contemporary Bible teacher and one from a more "old fashioned," conservative author.• The differences were nearly laughable--as were their examples. From studying these extremes, we were able to discuss not only the topics, but also the authors' approaches to these topics.

For example, from comparing both of their teachings, we discovered that their explanations of the verses concerning wives submitting to their husbands were so extreme and illogical, they were not even usable. In an effort to show the reader how outlandish a literal interpretation of the submission teaching is (without

•We are purposely not listing the titles of these two books. We are trying to show how we use books to develop our children’s thinking. We do not desire to be negative towards an author or his work.

considering other passages), the liberal author gave statistics on wife beating and abuse in Christian homes. He ended with a story describing one woman who was being abused but was told by her pastor that she was probably provoking her husband, followed by his beating her to death. Now, we found that the statistics about pastors telling women that it was probably their fault they were being abused, that they should not do anything about it (i.e. not leave for a season, not have the husband approached by the elders, etc.) seemed accurate and were alarming. However, to link even those logical statistics with Christian wives submitting to their husbands as causing wife beating was simply "non-linkable." In debate, we call this a "slippery slope." In essence, it is saying that because something happened once as a result of a certain cause (for example, sickness from seafood you ate last night), anytime that cause is present, it will happen again (i.e. every time you eat seafood or everytime you eat at that restaurant, you will be sick).

On the other hand, the conservative author used equally outlandish examples, citing that when women got outside jobs, they quit submitting to their husbands, and they often ended up having affairs and leaving their families. We believe there is some truth in women being under the authority of ungodly men with evil motives and in women putting too much emphasis on outside careers rather than reaching people for Christ and spending the time needed in their marriage and parenting leading to misplaced priorities, and sometimes even infidelity. However, the link cannot be made from this "submission teaching" to women working and leaving their families. Just because there is a negative outcome when someone does something does not justify saying that it is something that should never be done or else. Again, another slippery slope was presented.

We gained much from this study, and both authors actually made some valid points that we investigated further. However, reading the two extremes supplied us with examples of misusing Scripture and making applications that are simply not in the Bible. We have continued to discuss when we see this and when we ourselves are guilty of it. It has made us all stronger Christians, more godly women (well, not Ray!), and better Bible "scholars."

INGREDIENT #2: RULES WITHOUT RESPONSES

The second ingredient in the recipe for rebellion is that of rules without responses--developing rules without allowing our children to question those rules. This is a common ingredient in home-schooling, rules-oriented families. We often do not listen to our children if they disagree with something or question something.

No Response Is Aggravating!

There are many problems with this ingredient, of course, not the least of which involves the verse in the Bible that tells fathers not to aggravate their children: "Fathers, don't aggravate your children, if you do they will become discouraged and quit trying" Colossians 3:21 (NLT).[2]

It is aggravating not to be listened to! Think about how annoying it is for you with work or relatives when you are not allowed to voice your opinion. Your children feel the same way--only perhaps even more helpless because they are, well, children.

No-Response-Allowed Handicaps Our Children in Their Future Decision Making

Additionally, not allowing your children to respond to your rules and choices for them causes them to be unable to make decisions for themselves later in life. They need to know the process a Christian goes through to determine how to live and act. If we consistently tell them that this is the way it is, and they just need to buck up and do it, they will not learn how to make wise decisions for themselves and their own families some day.

No-Response-Allowed Is Not How God Treats Us!

Also, that is not the way God treats us! If we truly want to follow a Christian protocol in parenting, we will want to try to parent our children like God parents us. God listens to us!

Think of how painfully honest David was in the Psalms--*God, why are you doing this to me! Why don't you listen to me? Why do you let my enemies overtake me? Oh, I want to follow your way, but it is so hard. Okay, God, I will trust in you, not in chariots and horses.* God allows us to respond to what he is doing in our lives!

Or how about Abraham: *Will you destroy the city if there are some godly people still there?* He not only responded to God's edict, but he gave God suggestions on how to change it. And God listened!

Presenting a Godly Appeal

Most parents, when presented with the concept of letting their children respond to them, are not altogether wrong in their opposition. Their children might already be responding--and Mom and Dad do not like it! They usually do not like it because they have not allowed (or taught) proper responses from their children early on, so their sons and daughters have resorted to arguing, bickering, and begging. That is not the type of response we are recommending in this advice.

If you want to begin eliminating this ingredient from your rule-making and standard-implementing, we recommend that you utilize the godly appeal process.[3] In a nutshell, it is based on models in Scripture in which godly appeals were made and recognized. This approach still works in our families today.

In the godly appeal, if a child does not agree with something, he asks respectfully if he may appeal. We had our children use those exact words: *May I appeal?* At that time, the parent decides yes, no, or later. The child then must accept that answer (not argue, beg, etc.).

If the answer is yes, the appeal is heard and considered by the parents. Sometimes this is in front of other siblings. Many times it is not, depending on the subject being appealed, who it applies to, and the intensity of the child's appeal. If the answer is no, it is dropped, though it may be brought up later, when more information is gathered. If the answer is later, the child may bring it up at another, more convenient, time.

There are some guidelines that make the godly appeal successful:

1. If the appeal is disrespectful or done in anger, it is turned down immediately.

2. If the appeal is a series of whines and complaints, rather than a truly godly appeal, it is turned down.

3. If a child begins disagreeing a lot or constantly trying to appeal, the appeal process is terminated for a period of time until that person learns to accept Mom and Dad's rules more often than not.

4. If the appeal process becomes an argument, it is ended.

5. If the person appealing is turned down, but later has more information ("new evidence"), he may re-appeal that topic.

6. The appeal is truly listened to and thought through by Mom and Dad. Do not pretend to listen to appeals, but not regard your children's pleas. This is another recipe for rebellion in itself. (Kids know if the appeal process is just a formality and you are not truly listening to them.)

7. The person appealing is not constantly interrupted by Mom and Dad with justifications. The child should not be patronized during an appeal, but carefully listened to and respected.

The appeal process is a privilege for mature children. It should not be used by children who complain and grumble all of the time. It should not be used as a "formal means" of arguing. (The words, *may I appeal*, should not be substituted for the child's normal means of disagreeing, as an attempt to begin "discussion and arguments.") A child should have godly character and be characterized by ("known by") submission and obedience in order to utilize this relational tool. It is an avenue by which children and teens who readily accept the family's rules may disagree respectfully and be heard.

INGREDIENT #3: RULES WITHOUT REPETITION

The third ingredient in the recipe for rebellion is rules without repetition. This ingredient deals with inconsistency in applying rules. It points to the times our children comment, "Last time you let me." It means that when a rule is a rule, it remains the rule (unless it is truly, permanently changed, and then the change is enforced on a consistent basis).

Inconsistency Hinders Many Areas

Inconsistency will hinder a Christian in every area of his life. Our testimonies, relationships, interactions with others, decisions, morals--everything in our lives--must have some semblance of consistency in order to be accepted by others.

A young lady recently told one of my daughters that her parents are so inconsistent that she simply doesn't know what they want. One minute, she is allowed to date. Then when she begins dating someone they do not like, she is not permitted to go anywhere in a car with a boy. Inconsistency in rules will "provoke our children to wrath"[4] almost quicker than anything else.

The guidelines we have for our family's lifestyle must have consistency in order for children to follow them. Our schedules need consistency, or our children will never heed them--since they will change on a whim anyway. Our interactions with other believers, especially non-homeschoolers, must be built on consistency, too. People are watching us all the time. They judge homeschooling, and in many cases, the Christian faith, by our homeschooling decisions.

Inconsistency Creates Poor Testimony

I recently heard a sad commentary on homeschoolers from the director of a learning clinic in our area. She told a homeschooling mom that she knew that this mom was truly trying to help her son who had learning disabilities--that she knew this mom was not one of those "Wal-mart homeschoolers"! When questioned further, the director said that "Walmart homeschooler" is the term she and her instructors use for a homeschooling mom who brings her child to the learning center for help because the mom is at Wal-mart (or elsewhere, shopping and running around) everyday instead of actually homeschooling.

What a negative testimony we have with inconsistencies such as that. When we are known for not doing the job that we claim to do--not doing the hard work of homeschooling consistently and excellently--we disgrace homeschooling and cause people to distrust our decisions and disrespect us as homeschooling teachers.

With our children, it is even worse. Our inconsistency causes confusion, anger, and bitterness. Just like the girl told my daughter: "One day it is this rule, and the next day it is something different." Our children will not respect our rules if they are not consistently followed--or if the reason for a rule is not consistent in developing other rules (i.e. "one day I can date, the next day I can't be in a boy's car even with others there").

It should be noted here that we do not believe that consistency in making and following rules means that you cannot change rules. You may decide to change a rule: through God revealing something to you; through a friend pointing out a blind spot; through discussion with your spouse; or even through the appeal process. Consistency does not mean that you never change anything. However, when a rule is changed, your children need to know it is so, and you need to be sure to be consistent in applying the "new" rule.

INGREDIENT #4: RULES WITHOUT RELATIONSHIP

I will not spend a great deal of time on ingredient number four since it is covered in length throughout other parts of this book. Relationship must be in place in order to have a well-trained heart. However, I will note that we can chisel away the relationship we do have with any of the above three ingredients in our rule making. Even if we have a strong relationship in place with our children and have secured their hearts, we can cause them to take back pieces of their hearts little by little when we do not have logical rules, do not listen to them, and do not have consistency.

Likewise, an incredibly strong relationship can cause our children to accept our decisions even if we do not have some of the other three ingredients. If our children know that we are trying to do what is in their best interest, and that we would not simply make rules to throw our weight around, they will more easily accept those times when our rule making is less than logical or consistent.

Part II: Examples of the Four Ingredients of the Recipe for Rebellion From Our Family

I will give you examples of how we have applied this "recipe" in making rules in our home and the result of those applications in this last section. From these, as well as other times we followed the "Recipe for Rebellion," we have determined that some of our rules were not biblical, were man-made, were illogical, or were inconsistent.

The rules in these examples are not bad rules in themselves. The reasons they were bad rules for us is because we made them based on isolated Scripture verses (not considering other similar verses); we were inconsistent in applying them; we were hypocritical; we didn't allow the children to respond to them; etc. If you have these rules in your home, we are not suggesting you drop them. We are suggesting that when you have rules in your home, you give logical reasons for them, if possible. And that your rules, whatever they may be, do not contain the four ingredients in the "Recipe for Rebellion."

EXAMPLE 1--RULES WITHOUT REASONS AND WITHOUT REPETITION: DRESSING AND MODESTY

The following is an example from our parenting in which we lived out two of the ingredients for rebellion: *rules without reasons* and *rules without repetition*. In this case, we had Scriptures for our reasons; however, they were inconsistently followed (lacking repetition) and had illogical reasons (not logical when carried out fully). Remember, "rules without reasons" doesn't mean you don't have a reason at all--sometimes you have reasons, but they are illogical, which is the same as not having reasons at all in many ways.

A few years ago, our daughters and I primarily wore dresses and skirts. We were in a homeschooling group in which this was the norm, so we did the same most of the time. However, it was not a hard and fast rule for us as I often felt the inconsistencies in it.

We did not have a lot of reasons for this rule; we had just two Bible verses that we applied to this rule:

1. Not wearing men's clothing: "A woman shall not wear any thing that pertains to a man, nor shall a man put on a woman's garment, for all who do so are an abomination to the Lord your God" (Deuteronomy 22:5 NKJV).[5]

2. Covering the body more to keep from defrauding: "For this is the will of God, your sanctification; that you abstain from sexual immorality; that each of you know how to possess his own vessel in sanctification and honor, not in passions of lust, like the Gentiles who do not know God; that no one should take advantage of and defraud his brother in this matter..." (I Thessalonians 4:3-6a NKJV).[6]

Our reasons for the rule of wearing primarily dresses and skirts had several logical and hermeneutical difficulties that we discovered. It was a rule without logical reasons and a rule without repetition (in that we did not wear dresses and skirts all of the time, just most of the time).

Follow me through our reasons and logic and their breakdowns for this particular rule:

1. The verse we used to make this reason (not wearing any thing pertaining to the other gender) is in Leviticus, sandwiched between other verses about what the Jews should and should not eat, drink, and wear.
    a. Leviticus is a book of laws for Old Testament Jews, not necessarily a "rule book" for today.
    b. We do not follow other verses in that same book, like not wearing two types of fabrics together at the same time or letting our fields rest from planting every seventh year.
2. We did not follow it consistently.
    a. If we truly believe that this verse should be a rule for us, then we can never wear anything the other gender wears.
    b. Thus, we females would not wear polo shirts and tees--as these are "men's" clothes.
    c. We would quite possibly not wear denim (even in skirts) since denim was originally designed for men to wear for work.
3. If it is a rule, it is a rule, and we would never wear anything but skirts or dresses.
    a. Thus, we would not wear jeans while cleaning out the eavespouting or hiking.
    b. We would not wear sweat pants around the house, then change into skirts when we run errands.
    c. If it is a rule, it would have to be a consistent rule--if it is wrong to wear clothes of the other gender (and you believe pants are "men's clothes"), it is always wrong, not just when you are out.
4. The other reason for wearing primarily dresses and skirts, that of defrauding, was taken out of context in our case, as well.

a. We were applying that verse to something we already believed. In other words, we already believed that wearing skirts and dresses was superior to wearing pants and jeans, so we took that premise (skirts are better) and said that the other clothes (pants and jeans) defraud.

b. To use this verse as our reason for wearing skirts and dresses only, we would need to follow it through to other areas of dressing, as well.

    i. We would need to take this even further in order to keep from ever defrauding.

    ii. If we truly believed pants and jeans reveal too much of the female form to the point of defrauding, then the logical conclusion would be that most tops reveal too much of the female form and that some type of apron or covering should be worn over the top (much like our German Baptist and Amish friends do) to keep from defrauding as well.

If we had other reasons besides those two verses, it would possibly have been a good lifestyle choice for our family. For instance, many who wear only dresses feel that, in addition to those verses, it is also more feminine. Some believe it looks nicer to dress in dresses and skirts only. We know many who have this as their family's lifestyle guideline, and they have reasons for it that are logical and consistent to them and their children.

Others have additional reasons for making this rule part of their family's life, and that is fine. However, we believe that if a rule contains ingredients from the Recipe for Rebellion, it can lead to serious parenting and relational problems.

I should note here that our daughters never asked if they could not wear dresses and skirts. For some odd reason, they just did what we wanted them to do and what Mom did. However, I believe if we had continued in that manner as they got into their upper teen years, they would have questioned it because they would have spotted the lack of logic in our reasons, especially after a few years of debate training and Bible study at college.

EXAMPLE 2--RULES WITHOUT REASONS, WITHOUT REPETITION, AND WITHOUT RELATIONSHIP: NON-CHRISTIAN MUSICIAN

Another rule I made several years ago involved music. As an older teen, Joshua got a cd collection of Disney movie songs. Upon closer examination of it, I discovered that Elton John had written and performed many of the songs. Now I knew from my teen years that Elton John had lived an immoral life, and to my knowledge, was not a Christian. I forbade Joshua from listening to this (we even had him get rid of it entirely) because it had such a blatantly non-Christian artist singing some of the songs.

The problems with this rule were the inconsistencies, lack of repetition, and lack of relationship:

1. The verses that I found for my rule were applied incorrectly. I had a book about why contemporary music and rock music were wrong--and it listed reasons with Bible verses like some of the following:
    a. Contemporary music is addictive, with the verse "My son, incline thine ear to my teaching"
    b. Contemporary music has a bad beat, with the verse "Flee from evil"
    c. Contemporary music causes rebellion. with the verse "Heed my instruction, my son." The verses simply did not match the reasons.
2. We watched movies written by non-Christians, read books

written by non-Christians, studied art created by non-Christians, and much more.

   a. If my "he's not a Christian" rule was to work, we would have to eliminate anything not done by a Christian.
   b. Thus, we would not use practically any Christian literature course as nearly all of them study the "greats" in literature, Christian and secular.

3. My kids did point out number two above to me, and I said that they might be non-Christians, but Elton John was known for his ungodly lifestyle (during my youth; I am unaware of his lifestyle at this time).
   a. Of course, this logic could not stand up because many artists and classical composers (who were okay to listen to according to our rules) lived ungodly lives.
   b. Many of these composers are ones whom we had been taught to listen to because they were classical composers--and classical music was more accepted than contemporary music in many circles.

Now, if we had other reasons for these rules, or if we just felt the rule was right, but we were not sure why, and we told our children that--that is another story. But instead we had poorly applied Scripture (rules without reasons); we had illogical thinking in that he was more of a "non-Christian" than other non-Christian artists and authors (rules without logical reasons); we had no consistency in our rule--reading non-Christian authors (rules without repetition); we did not listen to our kids when they tried to discuss it (rules without response); and we built walls between Joshua and us due to those ingredients (adding the ingredient of "rules without relationship").

Again, there are many families we know and respect who do not allow any music in their homes besides classical and sacred music, and they have rules that their children accept and understand concerning this guideline. It is not the guideline/rule itself that made this not work for our family. It was that we did not have logical reasons, consistency, and openness about the rule that made it a problem.

RELATIONSHIP AND INTIMACY

Relationship and Sincerity Will Cover a Multitude of Parenting Lapses!

There have been times we wanted our children to do certain things, but we really weren't sure why. We just had a feeling about it. There is nothing wrong with this either--if we are honest with our children, and more importantly, that heart relationship is already in place.

For example, for most of my older kids' school years, I have not allowed the children to read or watch fantasy works involving witches or magic. There are many verses about staying away from these things, and I felt it was wrong to read these books or watch these movies. After much discussion for years and years with the older children, they have convinced me that there is a difference between casting spells for evil (i.e. Harry Potter) and using it for symbolism and that fantasy is simply make-believe, like Mickey Mouse or Winnie the Pooh.

I have come to let the children watch and read *The Chronicles of Narnia*, fairy tales, and other modern-day fantasy stories; however, I am uncomfortable with JR Tolkien books and movies, which are not that different from Narnia or other movies I do let the children watch. My older children (*older* being a relative term based on their maturity and acceptance of our rules) are free to follow their own convictions in watching and reading these things, but my younger children do not watch or read Tolkien, simply because I am not comfortable with them doing so.

It is not a big rule or regulation. Mom just doesn't know what she believes about it, and would rather you not. Once the kids reach a certain maturity in their relationship with the Lord and acceptance of our rules, they are free to watch and read Tolkien. The kids know I do not make rules unnecessarily; I don't say that everything that someone watches or listens to is evil; I enjoy entertainment too. I don't claim to always be right. They know I am willing to discuss these things with them and listen to their opinions. And they know that I only do what I see as best for them at the time. In essence, we have developed the relationship, so they accept the rule.

Antithesis of Rules for Rebellion: Ingredients for Intimacy

We have found a truly successful recipe for rebellion--with four key ingredients. We know exactly how to create the dish known as rebellious children. If the final product we desire is rebellion, we can follow this recipe, including the correct portions of those ingredients, and get a sizzling menu of rebellion--and, along with it, the inability to get into our children's hearts to train them.

Likewise, the opposite ingredients of the Rules for Rebellion can be combined to create a dish known as intimate relationship. If we give our children logical reasons; let them respond to us when they disagree; be consistent in making and applying rules; and develop deep, heart-affecting relationships with them, we can create the opposite of rebellion in our homes. We will then be following the Ingredients for Intimacy--and create an atmosphere where true heart training can transpire.

"Recipe for Rebellion"
Discussion/Application Questions
-- Chapter 7 --

1. Do you believe the recipe for rebellion is a valid recipe? Which areas do you disagree with?
2. If you find yourself reacting to the recipe for rebellion, thinking that you are the parent and they are the children--and they should obey and listen to you--spend some time praying and discussing this with a non-biased party and/or your spouse. How does God treat you?
3. Can you think of rules you have made that do not have logical reasons? Can you think of more logical reasons for these rules or should you eliminate this unnecessary or illogical rule?
4. When you use a Scripture for your reason for a rule or lifestyle guideline, is it accurately used? Are there other verses that say the same thing? Is the verse speaking to you or to another culture or people group (like in Leviticus)?
5. Can you think of something you have recently read or heard in which a Scripture was used and then extra-biblical and often unreasonable links were made to it? How can you teach your children to evaluate things more carefully using the premise that a verse should not be given and then outlandish or illogical links made to it?
6. Do you agree that God allows us to respond to his rules and decisions for our lives? How do you feel about letting your children respond to you?
7. If your children respond incorrectly now, but you desire to let them respond to you, how can you train them in correct responses?
8. Do you believe in the godly appeal? If so, decide when and how you and your spouse will begin implementing this in your home to eliminate "rules without response."
9. Can you think of times recently in which one or more of your children said something that inferred that you were being inconsistent? That last time it was different than this time? How can you become more consistent in your rule making and enforcing?
10. Think of a rule (or more than one rule) of which your children are unhappy. Take it through the "ingredients" list in this chapter. Does it contain one of the ingredients in the Recipe for Rebellion? How so? Should it be changed or altered in some way?

EIGHT

You Gotta Have Stick-tu-a-tive-ness

Other Hindrances to the WTH

In this section of the WTH, we have pointed out the two most significant hindrances to living the well-trained heart life: misplaced priorities and making rules with the Recipe for Rebellion. The third most impacting hindrance in developing the well-trained heart is probably that of improper socialization, which warrants its own chapter in the final section of this book. In this chapter, we will detail various other hindrances.

While we do not want to set a negative tone for heart training, there are key things that we have done that have caused us to have success in this approach--and there are key things that we have found, through trial and error, to be definite hindrances to achieving our goals. Therefore, we want to present these hindrances to you all together here--though many of the antidotes for these hindrances are elaborated on throughout this book.

The following five hindrances (with their many "sub-hindrances") will be addressed in this chapter:

Hindrance One: Not Maintaining Priorities
Hindrance Two: Fear
Hindrance Three: Parents' Selfishness
Hindrance Four: Negative Influences on Children
Hindrance Five: Mean and/or Boring Parents

HINDRANCE ONE: NOT MAINTAINING PRIORITIES

Develop Accountability for Your Priorities

Ray and I have had unusual success in keeping each other accountable for our lifestyle. It isn't perfect by any means, but we do encourage one another on to good works daily. However, oftentimes that is not the norm. Most people do better with outside accountability. If you are one of those people, we highly recommend that you get that outside accountability.

Just be careful in choosing those in your life for accountability. It is easy to slip into mediocrity when those holding us accountable expect only mediocrity in their lives. No judging intended here; just telling it the way it is. We have a tendency to measure our spirituality by those around us. If someone near us is doing better than we are, we often find fault with him or steer away from him. If someone near us is doing less than we are, we often compare ourselves to that person, which makes us feel that we are better.

You Gotta Have Stick-tu-a-tive-ness

Obviously, there are some serious character and relational issues involved in those scenarios. Nonetheless, when considering accountability, find someone with similar priorities who will not excuse your negligence, but will actually call you on it.

Write Your Priorities on Your Calendar

If something is a priority, it will stick. It will be penned into the calendar just like a meeting at work or a class at church. Now, obviously, you can have flexibility to move things around according to your needs, but too much flexibility will result in squeezing out the most important things. Remember, it is easier to say no to those closer to you than to those outside.

We have weekly calendar meetings with our young adults. Everyone puts everybody else's schedules on their calendars. Then we write in the dates and times we will spend together: the family nights; the date times with Mom and Dad alone; the time the older ones will invest in the younger ones, etc. These are our priorities. They are in our calendars because they are important.

For example, when my homeschooling moms' group meets to plan events, I look at my calendar and say no to activities that would fall on times with our young adults. They are only available certain days and times, and those days and times are reserved for them--opportunities to be with them are our priorities, as much as possible.

Don't Allow Satan to Steal Your Time

Time. Where does it go? Well, as we know, much of it is wasted, squandered away in meaningless activities and pursuits. Additionally, time is stolen from--and we often allow it to be.

Time is stolen from us when we get to the end of our lives and realize, as surveys show, that we have spent thirteen total years of our life watching television. Time is stolen from us when we sit down to play hearts on the computer, and we look at the clock and realize that three hours have passed. Then we do the same thing the next evening and the next. Time is stolen from us when we get involved in a certain novelist and find ourselves reading his books for hours and hours week after week until at the end of the year, we have made it through all of them--and spent hundreds of hours doing so.

Time is stolen from us when we drive our children from one less-than-important activity to another, grabbing fast food, shuffling kids in and out, arguing due to the pressures and demands of the day, only to discover that an entire week has gone by and we have not prayed together, talked about spiritual things, trained our children in godly character, or read the Bible with them.

Do not allow Satan to steal the time that God has given you to accomplish your priorities! Live a purposeful life with your priorities listed--and choose the activities that fulfill those priorities.

Note: We are not "time gestapos," monitoring every second, making sure no fun seeps into our lives. We enjoy cuddling up in the winter with a romantic comedy and no kids for a few hours. Our children enjoy their individual recreational activities--following a favorite football team; collecting, sorting, and trading coins; watching movies; playing computer games; keeping up with friends on the internet; building with Legoes; playing sports in the yard. But, again, those types of things are free time activities--times to relax, rejuvenate, and re-connect after facing the difficult challenges of serving the Lord and others.

HINDRANCE TWO: FEAR

Fear of What It Takes to Hit the Target

When I was in college, I had to take six physical education courses, so one five week summer session I found myself in the midst of archery class. Now, I'm not exactly what one would call an athlete. And I'm especially not a fan of dangerous sports. I don't participate in baseball, softball, ice skating, paint balling, snow skiing, bungee jumping--anything that might cause physical injury to my person.

Anyway, one of my carpool friends was also taking archery that summer session on a different day and time than I was. She had her first meeting before my first meeting, and the day she came to our carpool after her archery class will forever be etched in my mind. She had gone to her 8:00 am archery session, pulled back on the bow as instructed (well, sort of), and shot her arrow off, only to have the bow spring back and whack her on the upper arm. A large portion of her arm was literally purple. And I was filled with fear.

The next day when I went to my archery class, I found myself unable to pull back on the bow the way I was instructed. It might spring back and hurt me. I would have a purple arm. I would be in pain.

So instead of shooting my arrow straight ahead at my target, I released it early, turned the bow slightly, pulled my arm back--whatever it took to ensure that the deadly bow string did not harm me. And I did that the entire five weeks.

Thankfully, I had taken the course as a pass/fail venture, and if we came to class each day, we passed--because I never once hit my target. Mind you, I'm not talking about hitting the center of the target. I mean the target itself. Now, you should know that I hit targets around me--the one directly to the left of mine, the one directly to the right of mine, and even a target two targets over. But I never hit my own.

I was afraid to do what it took to hit my target. My friend had tried it and gotten hurt. It looked too hard; it seemed too painful. I wanted to hit the target. I wanted to do what it took to reach my goal--but I was afraid of the process.

Sometimes we simply do not want to do what it takes to raise our children the way we know we should. It doesn't look easy, and the process is often riddled with inconveniences and difficulties. And we fear the pain of it all.

Fear of Failure/Fear of Being Different

At other times, it isn't pain that we parents are afraid of. We're used to pain--childbirth, having our heels run into with a grocery cart manned by a ten year old, etc. No, our biggest fear is often fear of failure.

We are afraid that if we determine our target and shoot straight at it, we will somehow fail. Thus, we look around us to others' goals. We shoot for theirs instead of ours. And sometimes we hit theirs--but we continue to miss our own.

Doing things differently can be daunting, I agree. And while I don't believe in making it our life goal to be as different and odd as we can be, if we want to train our children's hearts well, it will require many decisions and life choices that are different than the average Christian parent, and maybe even different than other homeschooling parents we know.

You Gotta Have Stick-tu-a-tive-ness

If we want to achieve our goal of training children's hearts well, we have to let go of our fear. We have to be willing to pull back on the bow with all our strength--and shoot straight for our target--without being influenced by those with different goals and priorities, without fear of what others will think if we choose a target that is different than others' targets, and without fear of the difficult and lengthy process.

This cannot be done on our own; nothing of eternal value can. We must search out God's promises, and pray that they will be fulfilled in us. God is more interested in our success in raising our children for him than we could ever be. We must trust him to provide all that we need to accomplish this task--and move forward to do whatever it takes.

HINDRANCE THREE: PARENTS' SELFISHNESS

We have addressed some areas of parents' selfishness and its effect on the well-trained heart approach in "Let It Begin With Me." However, it is so important to the success of training our children's hearts, that we will address more aspects of it here.

Most of us were raised in traditional homes in which we were encouraged to "look out for number one," "be all that we can be," etc. We grew up believing that "it was all about us," which makes it extremely difficult to live a selfless life as an adult--and especially to teach our children that it is not "all about them."

Just because we became Christians, had children, and chose to homeschool them, does not mean that we will automatically become self-less adults. It just doesn't happen that way. We have to make a decision each day to live selflessly as parents, even while we are trying to train our children to do the same. We have to continually and humbly submit ourselves to God and His will and ways in order to live a more selfless life that is worthy of our children's modeling.

Career, Hobbies, and Interests

Have I mentioned enough that there will be time later for us--for careers, hobbies, and interests? For nicer things and more leisure time? Well, there might be, but even if there isn't, what sacrifice is too great to bring our children into God's kingdom and disciple them to live selfless lives that reflect the character of Christ? Honestly, what career, hobby, sport, or interest could I possibly have that is more important than this heart training?

We are told over and over again in Scripture to train our children in God's ways. Then we are told over and over again to make disciples (bring others to Christ and teach His principles and ways). Living the well-trained heart lifestyle gives us the opportunity to fulfill both of these callings: train our children in God's ways and make disciples. Don't let lesser things get in the way of these callings!

Laxness of the Parents

More often than not, we know what to do; we know what it takes to reach a certain goal; we know what steps we need to take to get from here to there, but we are simply too lax to do what we know we should do.

There is no simple answer for overcoming laxness. Of course, we have the power of the Holy Spirit to help us live the Christian life and practice the fruit of the Spirit, but we have to choose to do the next right thing. We have to dig our heels into the resistance that comes when we aren't doing what we know we should be doing.

You Gotta Have Stick-tu-a-tive-ness

Everyone needs support. Carve out time in your schedule for extended meetings with the Lord. Create a "well-trained heart" support group. Get in a parenting group. Join your church's cell groups. Do whatever it takes to make yourself do what you know you need to do in order to reach your goals.

There will be days when you just can't face it. Days when you will not do the right thing. But those days should be few and far between--not the norm.

"Be not weary in well doing!"[1] There are many days when I am sure that I will not be able to maintain the level of discipleship and training in my three little boys that I have had in my four older children. Ten-more-years-plus sounds long. But I cannot let laxness and laziness side-track me from my goal--that of training my children's hearts well.

HINDRANCE FOUR: NEGATIVE INFLUENCES ON OUR CHILDREN

Children are bombarded with negative influences today; that is nothing new. However, there are many negative influences that we create ourselves; there are many other ones that we can at least control or defer until our children are older and more ready for them.

Temporal Goals for Children

Everybody wants the best for their children, but our idea of best and God's idea of best are not always the same. We have a tendency to get caught up in the temporal--good education, fulfilling career, comfortable lifestyle, etc.--instead of what God says is best for our children.

Now, we're not opposed to a good education, and we do not think God is either. We strive diligently to give our children a strong academic background based on their abilities, strengths, and bents. We're not opposed to our children growing up and having careers that fulfill them. We're not even opposed to our children growing up and having incomes that are comfortable. However, those are merely by-products of training their hearts well--not the primary goals.

We have to ask ourselves: *Why do I want a certain career for my child? Why do I want him to go to that college? What are my motivations in my shaping of this child's education and life goals?*

What are your reasons for wanting what you want for your child? Are they selfish reasons? Are they temporal? Do they have anything to do with his true purpose in being here--to serve God and others? In his *Raising Truly Great Kids* conference (and his book *Raising Kids for True Greatness*[2]), Tim Kimmel suggests that temporal goals should only serve to help our children live the lives God has for them:

> We're supposed to instill in our kids a heart of incredible greatness so they're overwhelmed with the love of God and they want to go out in their future to serve him, love him, love others, and care for others. That's our job. And then while they're at it, they can make a living...and all that other stuff.[3]

We educate our children well, so they can fulfill the purposes God has for them. We train them, or help them receive training, in careers so they can fulfill the purposes God has for them. We teach them to earn money and manage it, so they can fulfill the purposes God has for them. It is when those goals of education, career, and comfort become the primary goals that we lose sight of training our children's hearts well.

Things of This World

Wanting our children to have so many material things and be comfortable is often our selfishness being revealed. Could it be that our desire for "the good life" for our kids is similar to the rich young ruler who came to Christ? When we set our children up to want more and more, to love money, to desire things, we are leading them into the path of the rich, young ruler--who could give everything up for God but his money and possessions.

When thinking of teaching our children to want so many temporal things, I am reminded of Hudson Taylor. As a youth he gave up his bed and slept on the floor. He gave up his regular food for a diet of rice. He sacrificed in both of these areas in order to prepare to serve those in China that he would minister to when he was an adult.[4]

How could our children ever desire to give up things of this world to serve God when we bombard them with luxuries constantly? How could they give up their comfortable lifestyle, complete with their own bedrooms, dvd players, televisions, cell phones, i-pods, computers, four-wheelers, game systems, motor bikes, sporting clothes and equipment, cars, and more for a simpler lifestyle when we have trained them that they need those things in order to be happy?

Our own selfishness in desiring so much for ourselves and our children and giving them an appetite for expensive clothing and collections, toys and gadgets, vehicles and electronics, has the potential to cause our children to desire temporal things more than eternal things. We need to hold loosely onto the things of this world, and teach our children to do the same---in order to keep our hearts in tune with God's will and training in our lives.

I am not advocating a life of poverty or martyrdom; however, most of us have way more than we need, yet continually think we need more. We build this into our children. Even the most conservative homeschoolers get caught up in this. We await the next item in our collection, the next large purchase we can make, the next trip to buy new clothing--and we, without realizing we are doing it, cause our children to build their lives around things rather than Christ and others.

Lack of Protection

Our children need protection--and much more than we usually give them. We believe this is why Scripture points to giving the child's heart to the parent: it is vulnerable. It is easily attacked and hurt. It is easily deceived. It is easily broken. Quite simply, it needs to be protected.

We often do not think enough about the situations in which we put our children. So many negative, or less than ideal, situations for our children today are accepted, even by homeschoolers. This is an area we would strongly encourage you to re-think, to look at differently--that of putting our children in situations in which they are not emotionally, spiritually, or physically safe.

Not long ago, a mom told me about her young daughter, only in first grade, who was in a community play. She went on and on about the concerns she had for this little girl having to work from after school until midnight for several weeks in a row; about how tired the girl was; about how mean the director could be and how the daughter often ended up in tears; and then she conceded by saying that, that is just how it is in theatre.

It might be the way it is in theatre, in some places and times; however, it doesn't have to be that way for our children. Any of those scenarios that mom described was reason enough to not allow the child to participate, the greatest of which was probably the emotional damage done by an overbearing, mean, thoughtless director.

Some time ago, our daughters were in an activity in which some of the leaders were not well-trained in handling children. The girls often came home with stories of how grouchy the leaders were; how badly the children behaved; how the participants were not made to follow the rules; etc. One evening, our eleven year old came home, pulled her chair close to mine, and just sat beside me with her arms around me, not saying anything for several minutes. I questioned her as to what was wrong. She shrugged and answered that nothing was really wrong.

She finally spoke up with, "I'm so glad to be home. I love being home where there are rules, and we are made to do what we're supposed to do. And you and Dad don't yell and scream at us. I love knowing what I'm supposed to do and being made to do it."

We ultimately decided that the girls were too young to be with other peers so much in semi-unstructured situations. The emotional toll it was taking on them was too great. Our children need protection from situations that are emotionally too taxing on them, physically too exhausting to them, and spiritually too dangerous for them.

We cannot emphasize enough evaluating every situation you put your children in--from staying overnight with cousins at Grandma's to kids' club at church to community theatre. We are not the type of parents who think everything out there is bad, and children should never be in anything, but we do believe our children need a lot more protection than we give them, especially until they are late teens/young adults.

Television and Entertainment

There are two definite keys that we attribute to our having our children's hearts thus far: not having television and keeping our children with us most of the time until they were in their late teens. We will address the latter in the socialization chapter, and although we have mentioned television as a time robber in previous chapters, we want to over-emphasize it, okay?

When we were first married, one of our early mentors advised us not to get a television for the first year we were married. As I mentioned earlier, if we saw anything in someone's life that worked, we were willing to try it, so we did not get a television that first year. Actually, we went seven years without any television or video monitor. Then we got a television and vcr and now have a television (without the ability to get television programming) with a dvd player.

I could tell you how bad television is, but you already know that 80%-plus of what is on television is just junk. I could tell you what Gregg Harris said in one of his early seminars: *You only watch news and sports? Well, I got news for you, Sport; it's on every hour of the day!*[5] And how much more is that true twenty years later with cable, dish tv, etc. etc.? (My son recently related to me that the sports station now carries an international rock-paper-scissors tournament. We are never lacking for some sport to watch!) I could tell you that electronics often get in the way of relationships. But you already know that, too. We all do.

But instead, I will tell you that we believe that not having television has been a crucial part of the heart training of our children. Why? Simply because there was nothing competing for our attention. There were no favorite programs. No news to catch up on. No sporting events to cheer on. No late night viewing. Or my personal favorite: no game shows to conquer!

We literally have had thousands of hours more to spend with each other and our children than families who have television and have it on every day. I do know a handful of people who have television and watch it just a few hours each week, but those people are few and far between. Most people are like us--if we had it, we would watch it.

If you or your children watch more than a few hours of television each week; if television is controlling you instead of you controlling it ("...hurry and eat; our show is coming on..."); if you are regularly subjecting yourself and/or your children to things you know in your heart of hearts are spiritually or morally unhealthy, but you do it because it's on or you have become somewhat addicted to it; if you spend more time on television than you do discipling; if your marriage suffers because the husband watches sports or the wife watches her shows instead of enjoying communication and intimacy; we beseech you to get rid of it and focus on the heart training of your children and the deepening of your marriage.

The same is true for video and computer games. If your children play more than a few hours a week, you cannot expect them to enjoy more simple pleasures---reading, being together, talking, worshiping, serving. It just will not happen. Why would they choose to help the handicapped at church on Friday night when their newest video game just came out? Why would they choose to read a book when their X-Box is calling out to them and they can play as much as they would like?

I know the arguments that they are just children, and we can tell ourselves that for a long time--and before we know it, they'll be young parents themselves watching soap operas and playing game systems instead of training their own children. They are children--that's why they need us to help them make choices for their lives now--and give them tastes for things that are of eternal value, rather than letting them fill themselves with tastes for immediate gratification and self-absorption.

They will likely not grow out of their love for entertainment if they are choosing it constantly as children. We need to put entertainment in its proper place for our children and for us: entertainment is what we do to relax after we have worked hard for God and others. It is a reward for doing the hard things. It is not what we live to do.

Substitute You

Bill Gothard tells a story in his Basic Seminar[6] about a dad who removed the television from his home. In this story, the children asked what they would do now, what the dad would give them instead of the television...and the dad said..."Me." Thus began a series of heart-turning activities. Each day the children called their dad at work, wanting to know what they would do that night. The dad came home ready to serve and be with the children, rather than all family members gathering in front of the television.

Negative influence of television aside, we have found this man's advice to be true and effective. We began early in our children's lives saying no to many things. At first, we said no more than we needed to. We parented in fear, so we said no to anything that made us afraid that something negative would influence our children.

You Gotta Have Stick-tu-a-tive-ness

However, this dad's example is what I believe saved us from exasperating our children with our constant no's: we gave them ourselves. In the early years, we told our children many no's. But, unlike many parents with long lists of rules, we didn't just tell them no and tell them this is the way it is since we're Christians. We told them no, but gave them ourselves to replace those things.

No Santa Claus, but lots of holiday baking with Mom and delivering goodies to the nursing home. No television, but lots of game nights and family fun. No video games, but lots of kickball, silly string wars, and hide and seek in the dark with Mom and Dad. No friends overnight, but family slumber parties. No junk food ...well that one didn't last long. No youth group, but family hospitality--and parents who were cooler than their peers anyway!

HINDRANCE FIVE: MEAN AND/OR BORING PARENTS

Mean Parents

After reading in this chapter about the importance of not thrilling our children so much, you may be surprised by hindrance number five: mean and/or boring parents. While we do not think children need to continually be thrilled, we also do not think they should have to tolerate meanness from their parents--and think it is advantageous for heart training if parents are, well, nice.

We see it all the time. As I sit here today in McDonald's doing the final draft on this chapter, it is unfolding before me: A dad hatefully yelling at his three-year-old daughter to put her cookies down so she can put her arm in her coat. Continuous yelling: "I told you to get this on. Now do it before I make you wish you had." No suggestion that it would be easier to put her coat on if she didn't have food in her hands. No "I'll hold your cookies while you put your arm in your coat." No holding the coat open while she slides into it. Just a shaking of the coat in front of her, treating her like she is stupid because she has cookies in her hand and cannot figure out how to get her coat on.

Why Are They Like That?

A few years ago just before Ray and I were going to speak one evening, we asked the kids what they thought we should say that night. Sweet Kara, then thirteen, looked at us with gentle, serious eyes: "Tell them not to be mean." Then she went on to relate how she stood by and watched a friend's mom belittle the girl for no reason. She ended with, "Why are parents mean like that?"

Many parents think that the meaner, stronger, more brusque their voice and actions, the more immediate, more complete, and more often the obedience of their children will be. Sure, you can sometimes intimidate your children into obeying, especially when they are young. You can make them fear your wrath to the point that they do all they can to avoid displeasing you (though in many "mean" parents, there is no rhyme or reason to their meanness and lashing out, so children truly do not know how to keep the parent happy anyway). However, you will be doing no positive heart training. As a matter of fact, the opposite will take place: you will train them in hatefulness, bitterness, and anger.

What Are You Characterized By?

This is not meant to be a guilt trip. We all lose our tempers at times. We all become impatient with our children. We have already discussed that in the transparency issues of chapter three.

However, just like with our children, it is what we are characterized by that matters. Are you characterized by being mean? Are you known as an impatient, grouchy parent? That approach to parenting is the opposite of what the Bible teaches ("raise your children in the nurture and admonition of the Lord") and the antithesis of how God parents us.

Boring Parents

My children and I have a cheer that we do on weekends (and any time we feel happy): "P-A-R-T-Y, party-hearty at Mommy High!" Even Brieanna, Cami's twelve-year old "little sister" (in the disability ministry "big sister program") wheels through the house in her wheelchair on her weekends with us singing: "P-A-R-T-Y, party hearty at Aunt Donna High!" One thing I am not known as is a boring mom!

We mentioned the importance of replacing those things that you are removing from your child's life with something else, namely you. In doing this replacing, we have tried to create a fun, safe, loving atmosphere at home so that our children desire being home as much as or more than being elsewhere. We do not have to continually thrill them, but, at the same time, we want them to see that living the Christian life does not mean that you cannot enjoy life too--and that you cannot enjoy ministry, family life, and serving others.

Family Time

When our older children were little, we did not designate one night a week as a "family night." We were all together at home with our children at least four evenings a week, so every night was family night!

We had an evening routine we usually followed. We nearly always ate dinner together at the table and then all of us cleaned the kitchen while talking, listening to radio dramas, or memorizing/reciting verses and songs. (This is how our older children learned the Pledge of Allegiance, National Anthem, "My Country 'Tis of Thee," Lord's Prayer, and the Ten Commandments, to name a few.) Then we either gathered around the table for Bible study, character study, or discipleship-type read aloud; or we went to the living room for family worship--complete with rhythm instruments (tambourine, maracas, sand blocks, rhythm sticks, etc.). Following this, we worked together, played together, read together, and stayed together most evenings. It was imperative that we use our family time wisely because we had so little of it.

The point to this isn't necessarily what we did in the evenings, but the point is that we *had* evenings. We had the time to invest in our children--and to have fun--because we did not fill every day and evening to the brim with outside activities. Our children looked forward to evenings and often asked throughout the day "What are we doing this evening?" They liked doing things together. We *lived* together rather than just residing in the same house together.

Several years ago we moved into our little white house when we downsized our lives. I can still vividly remember the first evening in this house. All nine of us were in the living room together listening to radio dramas, each one doing his or her own thing. Our two older daughters had their newsletter for young girls (one of their ministries at that time) all spread out on the floor in front of them; Joshua had his sports cards in long rows; Kara had some little dolls out; two of the little boys had Duplos all piled up; Jacob was in his exersaucer; I was in a chair doing school planning; and Ray was helping the girls with their mailings. The three hundred square foot room was brimming over with people and projects, and I was feeling it immediately (on our first night there!). Suddenly Ray spoke up: "Now see, this is the way it's supposed to be--all of us together, not all in separate parts of a big house." He was as happy as a lark because there was no place for the kids to spread out to. I didn't disagree with him out loud, but I didn't agree either. It was a big adjustment for me to go from a huge kitchen, pantry, full basement, large living room, etc. to our new place. However, Ray knew something even then that the rest of us would not come to realize until many years later: this little house forced us to learn to work and play together better than ever before.

Place High Priority on Time Together

We place high priority (and spend quite a bit of money, compared to other expenditures like home improvement, household décor, hobbies, vehicles, and clothing) on family fun times--and the training and education of our children. We now have an official "family night," a night in which both girls are not at their ministries or college but are with us, and we all do things together. Sometimes it is as elaborate as a birthday dinner out and a play or a big fondue dinner party at home with the ten of us. Other times it is as simple as a bonfire in the yard with singing and talking or walking trails at the state park nearby.

Our younger kids are still "home grown" in terms of family time. We watch our calendars and strive to have all six of us (the four children still in school, me, and Ray) at home together three or four nights a week. (Even when the children go places, it is nearly always together, so they continue to have "family time" when they are working in the disability ministry or at a cast party.) We want them to enjoy being home enough that they do not constantly want to go, go, go. This gives us more time to invest in them spiritually and character-wise, but it also gives us more opportunities to tie those heart strings by playing and working together.

We have certain games that are "ours"--ones we reserve for when Joshua and Lisa are over; others that are "Brieanna game night games" (games that our friend Brieanna can play easily when she is here with us); ones we play when the two older girls are gone; etc. (And I am glad we played with them so much when they were younger, even though I thought I would never live through another evening of Chutes and Ladders or Junior Monopoly! We actually play games I like now.)

We also enjoy sports as a family. We have done some organized sports for the kids occasionally, but we have found that they take so much time (and rob us of our four evenings a week together) that we often substitute family sports for these organized ones. Again, we have certain sports we play when Joshua and Lisa are here (five on five basketball and a homemade game we call hand-ball) and certain things we do with just a few of the kids (namely football and kickball). We have invented and tweaked games through the years that allow olders and youngers to play together more fairly. And sometimes (like in the case of volleyball) the littles have to sit out.

Most of us like listening to talking books and radio dramas. Through the years we have done this while traveling as well as when we work together at home on projects. Additionally, some of us enjoy movies, and we often watch movies together. Again, it is not that we believe you should not have any "fun," but that all of life should be in its proper order--and that just living, working, and serving can be enjoyed too.

Discussion is another aspect of family life that we like. Actually, that our kids love. Professional football and politics are the topics for some of the kids and Dad. Movies and books are often discussed by many of us. Something heard in a sermon or on the radio are nearly always part of dinnertime discussion. And then, there's life. There are times when a discussion on one topic will spark another, and that leads yet to another. And before we realize it, we have talked for two hours. And we had fun doing it -- and invested in our children's hearts in the process.

Lastly, we have always enjoyed doing things with other families. Before we began writing so much, we used to have extensive hospitality times in which we would have another family (or families) over for the evening. Sometimes we all ended up gathered together for worship time. Other times we packed all of us into the living room and played large group games. Many times the kids would go down to the basement (in our old house) or out to the schoolroom and play or talk. I could go on and on about the skills, deference, thoughtfulness, and servanthood that were built from these hospitality times, but this section is on fun, so I will just say that all of us have a lot of fun during hospitality times!

Most hindrances to heart training can be avoided and/or controlled. We have to be pro-active in order to train our children's hearts well. When we see something hindering that process, we need to remove that hindrance. We must have stick-tu-a-tive-ness to train our children's hearts well.

"Stick-tu-a-tive-ness"
Discussion/Application Questions
-- Chapter 8 --

1. Do you find yourself constantly making goals but having trouble following through on the process it takes to meet those goals? How do you feel about accountability in your life?
2. Look at your calendar? What things are written there now? Are those the things you want to be your priorities?
3. Initiate some sort of system whereby you control your priorities (calendar meetings, family meetings, etc.). How can you encourage your family to pen in their true priorities and cross out the less important things?
4. Make a list of the ways you have seen Satan steal time from you over the past couple of weeks. How can you keep that from happening the next time?
5. Do you find yourself fearing man? Do you understand deep down the importance of fearing God and not man? How can you turn your fear away from man and onto God, resulting in doing what God wants you to do rather than what others expect?
6. In what ways are you selfish with your family? List these and decide with God's help to rid your life of these selfish actions one item at a time. Develop accountability to be sure it happens, if needed.
7. Do you find yourself growing weary in well-doing? What can you do at the beginning of each day to find the strength to keep doing what you know God wants you to do? An email prayer partner? A phone accountability partner? Praying with your children for strength?
8. How have temporal goals of success hindered you in your heart training? Do your children feel that their future success in business and academics is more important to you than their spending their life serving God and others?
9. Do you find yourself consistently wanting more and more things? Being driven by a passion to have what others have? How can you turn your attention from worldly possessions to eternal pursuits?
10. Do you feel like your children are controlled by the desire for things-name brand clothing, pieces of collections, games, and toys? If so, how can you turn this around? How does spoiling them in those things affect their passion for God and simple pleasures of serving others?
11. What needs to be removed from your family's life in order to live a well-trained heart lifestyle? What can you substitute positively for those removed aspects?

NINE

"I Want an Oompa Loompa Now, Daddy!"

Avoiding a Child-Controlled Home

In the original movie, *Willie Wonka and the Chocolate Factory,*[1] an extremely naughty girl finds herself in a lot of trouble because, quite frankly, she is spoiled rotten. She asks for everything, and if she does not get what she wants when she wants it, she throws a ten-year-old tantrum. Her indulgent father continuously gives in to her demands, even to the point of trying to convince Mr. Wonka to sell him one of his Oompa Loompas, the pint-sized candy makers from Loompa Land, for his dear Veruca as she cries out, "I want an Oompa Loompa now, Daddy!"

CHILD-CONTROLLED HOMES

What Is a Child-Controlled Home?

Having a child-controlled home does not sound that terrible in itself. After all, if we have children, shouldn't we center our homes and lives around them? Believe me, I am all for sacrificing and centering my world around my children during the child-rearing days--taking the time and energy that is needed to raise them properly for the Lord. However, taking our responsibility to raise our children properly and focusing several years of our lives on their upbringing is significantly different than having a child-controlled home in which the children, not the parents, dictate things.

In the child-controlled home, where and what the family will eat, what is watched on television or at the movies, what a child will wear, and all the plethora of decisions that are made each week in a family's life are made by a child--or children. Oh, it isn't that the children are the authorities. It is just that because the atmosphere of the home is so influenced by the children's responses to every decision, those decisions are made in such a way to keep the children happy--to keep them from throwing fits, complaining, whining, rolling their eyes, sighing, pouting, yelling, and arguing.

At times it can seem so insignificant that a parent hardly notices that a child is running things. Jenny likes this. And Jenny wants that. And Jenny likes it when we do this. And Jenny has to have that. And the next thing you know, the home is controlled, in large part, by "Jenny." Suddenly, the parent (especially the mother) is afraid to make a decision that she knows Jenny will not like. And that family has a Jenny-controlled home.

Child-Controlled Homes Everywhere

Nowadays, children controlling their parents seems to be a natural occurrence. It is joked about on talk shows, from church pulpits, in beauty parlors, and at doctors' offices. Nobody seems to know what to do about the fact that children, not parents, often call the shots.

I Want an Oompa Loompa Now, Daddy!

Recently I was in a mall during the daytime when I overheard two young mothers talking to each other and their preschool children. One of the mothers told the children to come along because they were going to get a snack. The second mother questioned her, wondering if they were having lunch or a snack because they had planned on eating lunch. The first mother responded in a whisper with, "Oh, yeah, we're having lunch. I just tell my kids we're having a snack because if they think we are having a meal, they won't come to eat."

As I was thinking to myself about today's state of parenting in the secular world, I overheard a similar exchange soon after between a Christian mom who writes a marriage and parenting column for a Christian publication and her friend. In line at McDonald's, this gal asked her friend what her six and seven year old children were getting in their Happy Meals. She continued, "I have to be sure to get my kids exactly what your kids have in their Happy Meals or everything will break loose."

Why do parents (and especially Christian parents) walk on egg shells with their children? Why are they afraid to "cross" them? Why are they weak and unable to set the rules and guidelines for their family?

Even more important to our purposes, why do Christian homeschooling parents allow their children to rule their homes? It is amazing to me that a mother can face getting up in the mornings to school her children all day, knowing that if her children do not get their own way, there will be havoc.

The World's Parenting Philosophy vs. The Bible's Parenting Philosophy

The world, via the media, secular parenting specialists, fellow parents, and others, tells us that we cannot have proper control of our children. It paints a bleak picture about parenting children: try to stay firm on the battles you know you can win, and let the others go. (And the battles that the “experts” say you can win are few and far between.)

Do we have to go through our children's growing up years wishing they would behave like we tell them to? Do we have to beg, cajole, or bargain with our children to get them to sit down at the table or be content with what they have? Can we ever really enjoy our children, or does every command from us have to result in a battle?

Clearly, Scripture paints an entirely different picture of parenting than the world does:

- It tells children to honor and obey their parents: "Children, obey your parents in the Lord, for this is right" Ephesians 6:1 (NKJV).[2]

- It tells parents to train their children: "Train up a child in the way he should go, and when he is old he will not depart from it" Proverbs 22:6 (NJKV).[3]

- It tells us to discipline our children before it is too late: "Chasten thy son while there is hope, and let not thy soul spare for his crying" Proverbs 19:18 (KJV).[4]

- It tells us to love our children: "Then they (the older women) can train the younger women to love their husbands and children" Titus 2:4 (NIV).[5]

- It even tells us that disciplining our children is loving them---and not disciplining them is hating them: "He who spares the rod hates his son, but he who loves him is diligent to discipline him" Proverbs 13:24 (RSV).[6]

Of course, this doesn't happen overnight, but neither did the child-controlled home. Obviously, if we start out being in charge from the beginning and train our toddlers and preschoolers in obedience, having school aged children, and then teenagers, who obey and love us has more chance of being a reality.

Who Makes the Decisions for the Children?

I can still remember vividly a time when we were trying to get a handle on Joshua's behavior. I was questioning biblical discipline and wavering some on whether more "modern" techniques might be appropriate. One time, during my doubting weeks, I called two-year-old Joshua to come to allow me to put on his coat. He didn't come right away. I remembered an article I had read in a parenting magazine about talking sweetly, telling him the importance of your "wish," acting nonchalantly about a child's disobedience, etc., so I tried it. I had his coat in my hand as I told him that I really needed him to come, so we could leave. I told him that if he didn't come soon, we would be late. I spoke in soft, syrupy tones. Then I sat on the couch and acted like it didn't really matter to me whether he came right away or not. Suddenly, I looked down at the coat in my hand and thought about what I was doing and realized how foolish it was.

Joshua was training me, rather than the other way around! There I sat on the couch, unable to leave, because my little one did not want to. I was allowing an immature preschooler to dictate our schedule.

In essence, that is what we do when we do not punish our child, but let him do things his way or do what he wants instead of what we want. We are letting someone without the needed maturity and wisdom make decisions about himself (ie, when to go to sleep, what to eat, what to wear, etc.). When our children are given to us as babies, they are foolish and unable to take care of themselves or to make decisions on their own. God expects us to take care of them and make decisions for them, not let them do it for themselves simply to avoid tantrums.

Of course, as we have pointed out throughout this book, we are not opposed to explaining why we want a certain behavior, but a child should not have to have an explanation in order to obey. I explain what I want and why to my child for two reasons: (1) to keep him from becoming exasperated; and (2) to give him something to put in his "moral bank" for future reference. These early explanations are the foundation for later character training.

LARGE FAMILY DISCIPLINE

Seven Children: Same Benefits for Child Training; Same Heartaches for Lack of Training

People often gasp when we tell them we have seven children. "Seven children? I can't make the two I do have listen to me, much less seven of them."

To which I reply, "Well, we didn't get them all at the same time. We had time to get used to and teach one before another one arrived."

It is often assumed that because we have seven children, we have seven times the amount of disobedience, disrespect, and discontentment that someone with one poorly disciplined child has.

First of all, it doesn't matter if you have one, seven, or twelve children; if they are disobedient and disrespectful, it still brings heartache to the mother and shame to the father, according to the Bible.[7]

Secondly, when you begin disciplining your children effectively from the beginning, or at least with the first two or three children in the case of a large family, it has far-reaching effects to your younger children. You set a standard for behavior in the older ones that has the potential to trickle down to the younger ones, assuming the older ones interact with the younger ones and the entire family spends a lot of time together. We actually have had to punish our ten and thirteen year old sons (our fifth and sixth children) about twenty-five percent of the amount that we had to punish our second child, who is now one of the most selfless young adults I have ever met. Of course, she wasn't selfless at ages two and three! (Note: I am referring to punishment here; training and consequences have definitely been more extensive with our younger boys than with the girls. Gotta love three cooperative, diligent, responsible girls in a row!)

Thirdly, yes, there is the potential for seven times the amount of heartache for parents of seven children as there is for parents of one child, but there is also the potential for seven times the amount of joy. We have chosen to focus on biblical, effective discipline so that the potential for those joyful, loving, less problematic times is increased exponentially.

Perfect Children?

Children are never perfect--and I do not want to paint a picture that is unrealistic. Ray wouldn't have to tell me that we are "getting the behavior that we want" if our children were perfect! (Boy, I really don't like it when he says that!)

Some days, I go to bed weary and worried. How will we help our young adult daughter through the difficult time she is having? How can we turn a bad attitude around? Is a recent trend in one of the kids indicative of something much worse?

Even the most disciplined parents have problems. We are not guaranteed perfect children even if we do discipline and love consistently. However, the alternative that we see in the world--joyless, problem-saturated homes--is enough to keep me moving ahead in what I know the Lord has shown us.

SECURING A PARENT-CONTROLLED HOME

Taking Back Control

Many parents are bewildered as to how to take back their rightful place as, well, the parents. They feel overwhelmed with the consequences they will have to face if the child loses his or her control. Isn't it easier just to keep peace now and give the child what he wants? Maybe he will grow out of this selfish stage.

Proverbs 19:18 addresses this subject: "Chasten thy son while there is hope, and let not thy soul spare for his crying."[8] Wise words of Solomon--do it while there is still time, while there is still hope, leaving us with the impression that someday it will be too late. The Living Translation of this verse says that we can *ruin* our children by not disciplining them: "Discipline your children while there is hope. If you don't, you will ruin their lives."[9]

According to the KJV *Old Testament Hebrew Lexicon*, the word *chasten* here means "to instruct and to discipline." This is consistent with our thinking about the two aspects of "negative" (i.e. corrective) child training. Instruct indicates teaching (i.e. through verbal instruction and consequences), and discipline indicates what some call punishment or chastisement. The other words here are fairly literal--while there is still hope (before time runs out and it becomes a hopeless situation); he will not die (from the "chastisement").

Of course, even without that Proverb, we know in our hearts that this is true. We allow a baby to manipulate our home and schedule--at six months, nine months, twelve months--having to be walked around at night to go to bed, giving him our watch because he will not quit screaming in church until he has it (no toy will suffice), letting him determine our family's schedule. Then that baby becomes a demanding toddler--two year old who has to have his cup with the lid off or else. Then a preschooler, of whom nobody wants to be around. Into elementary school, a know-it-all, my-way-or-the-highway ten year old girl or demanding, pushy boy. Need I go on? Then the young teen, who is shunned even by his own siblings because his personality is so abrasive....and, well, you get the picture. We have to take back control now. Not later.

Wanting His Own Way

We have found the combined advice of James Dobson,[10] Gary Ezzo,[11] and S.M. Davis[12] to be a big part of the answer: *If a child is not happy when he does not get his own way, he should not get his own way.*

In a practical sense, this means that if our two year old screams because he has the blue sipper cup and he wants the red one, he is not mature enough to make that decision. He is unhappy when he doesn't get his way, so he should not get his way. And maybe this child should have the blue sipper cup for the rest of his life!

It means that if our four year old cannot share a toy with his brother, he is probably not old enough or mature enough to have that toy. It means that if our ten year old is not doing her assignments on time, she should not be the one who decides when she will do her home work, where she will do her home work, and what she is permitted to do until the home work is done. It means that if our sixteen year old cannot seem to get home on time after debate club, he is probably not mature enough to drive to debate club.

Bring in the Boundaries

One way that we have found to take back control of our children during times that we have felt that we lost control was to bring in the boundaries. When our children are not obeying, they are often being given too many choices and too much freedom. At that time, we have brought in the boundaries in different areas of their lives--and regained control.

For example, when a child is consistently unhappy with his meals, he should have less choices (not more to try to "make him happy"--regardless of the ever popular "Happy Meal"). We need to bring in the boundaries of his choices---just offer meat and vegetables or soup or whatever you determine until he is content and thankful for what he does have.

When a teenager begins displaying negative behavior like her peers, we need to bring in the boundaries that were broadened too much for her maturity. Lessen the time she spends with peers and discriminate more carefully which peers she should and should not be permitted to spend time with.

This is especially helpful with very small children. When we had a two-year-old who threw his food, would not eat what was put before him, and screamed in his high chair, we knew we had broadened his boundaries--his areas of control--too early. Those boundaries needed brought in. He was not obedient or mature enough to have his entire meal on his tray; he was not content enough to choose what he wanted from the dinner menu; he was not compliant enough to remain in his high chair for family worship; he needed removed from the family and placed in his crib until worship was over. His boundaries had been too wide.

Another example of this is when our older children would not keep the toy room picked up. We repeatedly told them to pick up when they were done with something, stop playing in plenty of time to clean up their messes, and not leave things lying around. However, they continued to leave toys strewn about in the toy room almost daily. The boundaries were too wide for them. They were unable to control themselves in the situation we had them in (i.e. an entire room of toys at their disposal). Thus, we cleaned the room with them entirely, then put huge sheets over ninety percent of the toys in the room. They were not to touch those toys, but could just play with the remaining ten percent of uncovered ones. Once they learned to clean up with that small amount, we uncovered another ten percent, then another, until they were mature enough for the boundaries to be widened to include playing with all of the toys in the room.

Releasing the Boundaries

Some might wonder if the boundaries will ever be widened fully in this approach. It may seem like your children (even teens) are not mature enough to allow the boundaries to ever come out in some areas. And I know that feeling.

There will be times when our children are moving into adulthood when we can no longer control their environments. We no longer have the options of bringing in the boundaries to help them gain control of themselves and their actions. At this point, many parents try to micromanage their children rather than releasing them to their own devices.

This is why we promote a gradual release of teens and young adults from under authority. The entire idea of the child turning eighteen and becoming an "adult" is simply inaccurate and damaging to young people. We have seen over and over again when a child graduated from homeschooling and was "released" without the proper guidance in his life. It was thought that "now he is an adult."

Yes, there will come a time when you will stop manipulating his environment to help him mature (stop bringing in the boundaries), and the child will flounder often. However, it should not be abrupt; it should be gradual. And it should not be without your constant input and guidance in his life even as a young adult.

Is It Too Late?

Many of you reading this might feel that you have blown it too badly in the area of parental control. You feel that no matter what you do now, you cannot gain it back. Re-read the section in "Debate" about appealing with love and the section in "Mom and Dad" about humility. It is not too late.

If you find yourself in this situation, humble yourself before your children. Explain to them that you feel you have truly blown it, that you have parented in such a way that they will not grow up to be godly, selfless, others-oriented adults. The self-focus you have allowed in them has the potential to produce failure as adults for them--as parents, as workers, as spouses, as Christians. Admit your own sins of pride and selfishness--that you, too, have been self-oriented, wanting your own way and responding incorrectly when it did not happen. Point out that we can only raise them to love God and others more than themselves if we take the focus off of them now. Then be certain to follow through.

If your children are older teens or young adults, do not go back and try to "control them" like you would a younger child. Simply admit that you failed in areas of discipline, ask for their forgiveness, and commit to them that you will try to get into their hearts and show them God's love and ways in spite of behavior problems. Do not put it back on them--let them know that you take responsibility for the problems--and that you love them in spite of behavioral and lifestyle issues.

Maybe they will not respond the way you hope, but your humility in the situation will go a long way toward them eventually understanding what you are trying to do. Relate to them in love. Tell them that you are not trying to strong-arm them into being or doing something that you are not willing to do yourself, but that you truly want to be the kind of person God wants you to be, and you want to help them become that kind of person too. Then love them back into submission. We know it is not as simplistic as it sounds on paper. We know that it is hard to be loving towards someone who is self-absorbed, but brow-beating them into submission will not work. Only love covers a multitude of sins.[13]

"I Want an Oompa Loompa Now, Daddy!" Discussion/Application Questions -- Chapter 9 --

1. Do you have a "Jenny" running your home? Write down instances in which your child or children control your home and decide together with your spouse to tackle these one at a time, until control is in its rightful hands.
2. What has your view of discipline been in the past? Do you firmly believe that disciplining your children is loving them and not disciplining is not?
3. What "modern" discipline or punishment techniques have you bought into? Do you see how these are counter to much biblical teaching on discipline? How have they hurt or hindered you in the discipline of your children? What more effective ways can you replace those with?
4. Do you feel the urgency to take back control before it is too late? Pray for the Lord's guidance and courage to follow through.
5. Which of your children, if any, have had the boundaries in some area of his life widened too soon? How can you pull in these boundaries?
6. Do you see the importance of humility and admission of your own part in your child's behavior problems? If you feel a need to approach your child about this, how and when will you do this?
7. If you and your husband agree that your children's behavior has been mismanaged, pray together to gain unity, and seek to turn that around together.

TEN

Spank, Rattle, and Roll

Child Training and the Well-Trained Heart

In the previous chapter, we outlined some steps to gain control of your home. Obviously, it is easier to have control of your home and children if you started out with it than it is to try to gain it later on. This book focuses much on the heart of the child--gaining it, holding it, protecting it, loving it, training it, turning it in the right direction, and releasing it when it is time. However, the heart training of our children begins with controlling their outward behaviors early on, when they are unable to control those behaviors themselves. Yes, this outward control by parents should decrease. There will even come a time when you can be that "buddy" that you wanted to be early on, though by that time it will not feel like a "buddy" relationship, but rather an adult heart-to-heart relationship. However, the early years are not the time for that.

Necessity of Parental Control

Reb Bradley, veteran homeschool father, author, and speaker addresses this phenomenon, and the eventual transition:

> Establishing strong parental control early on in life is necessary, because as our young children learn to submit to outer controls, they concurrently develop inner controls. And a young child who is trained to have inner control (self-control) is better equipped to receive values taught them as they grow.
>
> However, as our children head into adolescence, if we find ourselves still focused on influencing them chiefly through tight control, we shouldn't be surprised if they begin to manifest an independent spirit some time during their teens.[1]

That's why all the fuss about a parent-controlled home. That is why we should not "wait until later" to chastise our children. Again, children are given to us as babies for a reason--and during their childhood years, they are filled with foolishness. It is up to us to drive that foolishness out of them: "Foolishness is bound up in the heart of a child; (But) the rod of correction shall drive it far from him" Proverbs 22:15 (ASV).[2]

Obedience Is Better Than Sacrifice

As related earlier, we discovered that character had to be first in our child's life because someone gently pointed out to us that we had placed knowledge ahead of character with Joshua, our first-born.

Oh, how thankful we are for that early lesson. It became the basis for our entire parenting and home schooling philosophy: godliness before knowledge; character ahead of education; obedience instead of sacrifice; relationship over religion; and on and on. We still taught him the Bible and its principles, but we focused more on the application of the Word rather than learning (and showing off!) mere facts. Putting character training ahead of academics throughout his life didn't seem to hurt him: a couple of years ago he received a BA in history--after testing out of all but two classes that did not have tests available!

What's It All About?

This chapter will detail what we see as two major aspects of *corrective* child training. There are many sub-topics to these two aspects, so we will outline them for easier following:

Two Aspects of Corrective Child Training: Biblical Discipline and Consequences

I. Corrective Child Training Aspect One: Biblical Discipline
- A. Explaining Expectations
- B. Punishment
    - (1) Thank-You for Spanking Me
    - (2) Three Ineffective Methods of Punishment
        - a. Delayed Obedience or 1-2-3 Obey!
        - b. Threatening Without Following Through
        - c. Ineffective Gimmicks
    - (3) Disobedience or Childishness
        - a. Which Behavior Is This?
        - b. Obedience Math
        - c. Benchmarks for Determining Disobedience and Childishness

II. Corrective Child Training Aspect Two: Consequences
- A. Childishness
    - (1) Think as a Child
    - (2) Childishness Is Undeveloped Character
- B. Reality Discipline

(1) Basis of Reality Discipline
(2) It Just Makes Sense
(3) It Is Biblical
(4) It Is What Happens in Real Life
(5) It Requires a Balance of Grace and Justice in Implementing It
(6) Punishment and Consequences: No Easy Way Out

TWO ASPECTS OF CORRECTIVE CHILD TRAINING-- BIBLICAL DISCIPLINE AND CONSEQUENCES

I love what I have learned from Gary Ezzo[3] and Kevin Leman[4] about effective child training. They have helped me focus on biblical discipline (instead of fads or formulas) and reality discipline, or consequences (instead of ineffective gimmicks). While there is much more to training children in God's ways (such as encouragement and affirmation and other "affirmative child training" aspects), two of the major aspects of corrective child training for us are biblical discipline (called punishment or chastisement by some) and reality discipline (also known as consequences).

I. CORRECTIVE CHILD TRAINING ASPECT ONE: BIBLICAL DISCIPLINE

The first aspect of corrective child training, and the one most exclusively used in the first three years of our children's lives (from nine to twelve months up to three or four years) is that of biblical discipline. Some call this punishment or chastisement. It is actually more than punishment though. It is training a child in your expectations (i.e. don't touch) and disciplining (punishing) him properly when those expectations are not met.

A. Explaining Expectations

For us, the first step in biblical discipline has meant explaining what is expected in order to keep from exasperating our children. We have discussed this extensively in other chapters, especially the chapters dealing with older children and teens. However, the foundation of this is in the early years. Our children cannot follow rules or obey us if they do not know the rules or expectations.

We have taken this step to heart deliberately throughout our children's early years. Anytime we were going into a new situation from the norm for that day or time (i.e. on the way to the doctor or just before company arrives, etc.), we would explain in detail what was going to happen, what the atmosphere or situation would be, and what was expected of our children in that scenario.

For years and years as we were driving to an event in which other children would be there and the kids would be playing, we would tell them what we expected as we traveled: *Tonight there will be a lot of kids here, and Mr. and Mrs. Jones do not have small children, so they are not used to having this many kids around. It would not be appropriate to play knee football or some of the more active things you play with Daddy in the family room. It would be more appropriate for you to play quiet things like your Legoes or table games here. Of course, if there are toddlers there, do not get your Legoes out at all. Use Duploes instead.*

And for years and years we would always remind our children of the character and relational behaviors we expected of them each time we were going to be around others: *Who will be your best friends tonight?* (My brothers and sisters!) *Who will you protect and include?* (My brothers and sisters!) *Whose feelings are more important than anyone else's tonight?* (My brothers and sisters!) *Who has the best family in the world?* (We do!)

There was never a question as to what was expected in any social situation (unless something changed after we got there, such as the unanticipated arrival of a child with whom we were not comfortable or the kids staying with the parents when we had previously thought the kids were having play time, etc.). To the best of our knowledge, we prepared them so that they knew how to adjust their behavior according to the situation.

Again, some might question the necessity of this, but notice the last sentence of the previous paragraph: *so that they knew how to adjust their behavior according to the situation.* We were not just training them for the moment (though that was certainly part of it). We were training them for the long-haul. By preparing them for situations and giving them our expectations, we were helping them learn how to obey--and how to regulate their own behavior in future scenarios.

For instance, in the case of explaining to them that they should not rough house in Mr. and Mrs. Smith's home because the Smith's are not used to having young children there, we were training them for similar situations they might encounter in the future. It wasn't uncommon for us to hear one of our children repeat our teaching in another situation: *Now, remember what Daddy said about playing quietly at Mr. and Mrs. Smith's house last week? This is just like that. We should do calmer activities here because Grandma and Grandpa Rager are old, and they have a lot of breakable things.*

B. Punishment

The second aspect of biblical discipline in the early years is punishment for disobedience. This is where things get complicated. First of all, there is the question of appropriate discipline or punishment. Then there is the question of whether a behavior was disobedience or childishness.

We have believed in and practiced spanking as a means of biblical discipline for children from the beginning of our parenting. We do not have the space in this book to give a proper, thorough argument for our basis of this, but we have believed that when the Bible says "spare not the rod,"[5] it likely means that we should not shrink from spanking our children when they disobey. We also believe that when Scripture says not to avoid disciplining your child just because of his crying,[6] it is likely indicating that a child will cry because of being spanked.

Thus, we have explained our expectations to our young children through the years, then spanked them for disobeying us. Of course, it is not always as simple as that, but that is the basis of discipline for disobedience. Biblical discipline is not tricking, bribing, begging, screaming, hitting, threatening, or spoiling. Biblical discipline is giving a clear command, expecting it to be followed, and punishing when it is not followed.

(1) Thank-You for Spanking Me

We have always talked extensively to our children. We talked about their behavior, our expectations, their response, etc., but we also talked about other children's behavior, using these examples as teaching tools in the process. Thus, our children are, and have been since they were little, acutely aware of other people's behaviors.

One time when Cami was five or six, we were in the grocery when the typical "tantrum" occurred in our aisle. A little girl was throwing a fit because she could not have (at that time!) what she wanted.

She began screaming, crying, flailing her arms, pulling on her mom's clothes, and stomping. The mom continued to tell the child to straighten up, all the while dragging her along as she pushed the shopping cart out of our aisle and into the next. The fit continued into the adjacent aisle, with the screaming escalating so that it could be heard from nearly anywhere in the store.

Knowing we would discuss this on the way home, I continued my shopping only to have Cami come up to me, tug on my shirt, and reach up to put her arms around my neck. She hugged me tightly, and I soon realized she was crying. When I asked her what was wrong, she answered: "Thank-you for spanking me, Mommy. Thank-you for not letting me be like that little girl. I would hate it if I was allowed to act like that." And she held me and sobbed quietly while the little terror two aisles over continued wailing.

Disciplining children is the right thing to do. It teaches them obedience, submission, and personal responsibility. It gives them the tools that they need to grow up with self restraint. Some day, our children will thank us for it.

(2) Three Ineffective Methods of Punishment: Allowing Delayed Obedience, Threatening, And Other Gimmicks

Of course, if what we see as biblical discipline works in child training, there are obviously other methods out there that we feel do not work. Three methods of punishment that are not effective are allowing delayed obedience (letting children have time to decide to obey), threatening without following through, and other "punishment gimmicks."

a. Delayed Obedience or 1-2-3 Obey!

When Cami was just under five, we lived back a long, long lane out in the country. At the beginning of the lane lived a family with a boy who was also five. Occasionally, this little guy would come down to play with Cami, but he never wanted to go home when it was time.

One evening at dinner, after this neighbor boy had been down playing in the yard with Cami, she started to describe to the family around the dinner table his mom's disciplinary technique. Now I will forever keep this moment in my "mind's picture gallery."

Cami could barely get the first sentence of her news out because she was laughing so much, her eyes big and her sweet little hand covering her giggles, as she exclaimed:

"You'll never believe what Billy's mom does when he disobeys!"

"What?" we questioned.

"She....she...(giggle, giggle)..she COUNTS!"

Then she went on in great detail and with great animation to describe the scene to us:

"She told him it was time to get his bike and head home, and he said he didn't want to--like he always does."

(She's saying this all really fast yet matter-of-factly while giggling.)

“And she said he had to… and he said no again…and she said not to make her tell his dad…and he said no again…and then his mom looked real serious-- and she started COUNTING!! "

Giggle, giggle--what a dolly...

When she recovered from her giggling, she asked in complete seriousness, "How does counting make someone obey?" (Out of the mouth of babes, huh?)

We explained this child training technique to the children: When a parent begins counting, it means it's the last straw, and the child has to obey by a certain number or else.

Then she and her siblings began giving each other commands: "Put your hands on your lap," "Pass the salt," and "Give me your butter bread," then counting after the command was given to see if counting made a person obey. It was actually hilarious to see them, and it brought out the absurdness of counting to get obedience.

Of course, this led to a lesson on first time obedience and how Mommy and Daddy should never have to give a command over and over to get them to obey--and we should never have to count.

Biblical discipline is not game playing. We should give our children commands and expect them to obey them cheerfully. We should not have to resort to begging or bribing. When we realized that Joshua needed training in obedience more than he needed training in Bible facts, we began expecting him to do what we said. When he didn't do what he was told, he was punished for it.

b. Threatening Without Following Through

We all know about (and have all practiced) threatening without following through. Most of us can hear ourselves doing it and realize how ludicrous it is. We tell the child that "if you do that one more time..." or "if you don't get this done by such and such time, you are gonna be in trouble."

Of course, this is ineffective child training, but it is also exasperating to the child. He is left to figure out, on a case by case basis, whether you are serious or not, whether he will really be disciplined this time, or whether he can "get by with it" once more. We are essentially training our children to disobey when we threaten our children without following through.

c. Ineffective Gimmicks

Many "modern" parents have bought into some of the "modern" gimmicks of child training. Everywhere we go we see a child blatantly disobey a parent, then sit in a chair for five minutes. (*Hmm...that wasn't that bad; guess disobeying is worth it if that's all I get.*) We see a boy back talk his mom, then go do ten jumping jacks in the other room. (*Wow! Can I do ten more?)* We see a girl roll her eyes at her dad, and then get yelled at (and threatened). (And then roll her eyes again.)

We don't completely shelf the time out idea. It is actually a form of reality discipline: if you are socially improper, nobody will want to be around you. However, as a disciplinary technique for disobedience, time out is virtually useless.

We have found in our parenting that disobedience and disrespect are best turned around in a child by spanking the child. Not having him sit in a chair. Not having him lie in his bed. Not putting him in a laundry basket. Disobedience and disrespect are blatant acts of rebellion against Mom and Dad and should be disciplined with the "rod of correction."

(3) Disobedience or Childishness

In our child training, Ray and I have tried to determine whether a behavior was rebellion against us (as in outright disobedience or disrespect) or childishness (as in forgetfulness, procrastination, sloppiness, etc.). We do this because disobedience requires biblical discipline whereas childishness requires the second aspect of child training we have used: reality discipline (or consequences).

a. Which Behavior Is This?

Discerning between disobedience and childishness can be so difficult! Even after twenty-five years of parenting, Ray and I still continuously ask each other which behavior a child is displaying.

Difficult or not, we must do it. The Bible says that we are not to exasperate our children.[7] Two sure ways to exasperate them are to punish incorrectly, as in anger, etc., and to punish something as disobedience, when we should be training through consequences.

All parents are faced with this. A child dawdles when we call him to come get ready for bed, and we wonder whether this is just childishness or if it is real disobedience. When our son leaves the dog out of the kennel for the third night in a row, and the pooch potties on the new carpet, we ask ourselves if our little guy is disobeying or forgetting. Children *and* adults forget things, and need help remembering (usually with reality discipline, or consequences).

b. Obedience Math

When our older children were little, we taught them what we called "obedience math." It goes like this:

Obedience + Own Method = Disobedience
Obedience + Delay = Disobedience
Obedience + Incompleteness= Disobedience
Obedience + Bad Attitude = Disobedience

Obedience math sums up the saying, "Do what you are told, when you are told, how you are told, with a good attitude." Thus, obedience math is not childishness but outright disobedience.
It is not childishness when a child is given a direct command, and he does something different than he is told. It is not childishness when a child is given a direct command, and he waits and does it on his own timetable. It is not childishness when a child is given a direct command, and he only does part of the command. It is not childishness when a child is given a command, and he complies but does it with a bad attitude. All of those are disobedience and should be punished.

c. Benchmarks for Determining Disobedience and Childishness

Through our years of parenting seven children, we have established a few benchmarks that have helped us determine if a behavior is disobedience or childishness.

One benchmark is the age of the one violating the command. If I tell my seven-year-old son to go unload the dishwasher right now, and when he comes into the dining room to put some knives away, he starts watching his brother play a computer game and forgets about his dishes, he is being childish. Seven year olds get distracted! He doesn't need severe punishment for his infraction. He needs reminding and, perhaps, consequences, if he is characterized by getting sidetracked by computer games.

However, if my fourteen year old is told to go take the trash to the corner and then come back and help his brothers straighten the family room, and he stops to shoot baskets for fifteen minutes, he is more than likely disobeying. He should be mature and responsible enough by that time to consider his brothers' feelings as they do his portion of the work. He should be obedient enough to go do the job he is told, then come back inside and do the next job.

Another benchmark is whether the violation was of a direct command just given or a routine or schedule type command. For instance, when I tell my seven year old to go unload the dishes right now, and he decides he would rather go upstairs to play Legoes, he has directly disobeyed me and needs to be punished. However, when he finishes his morning routine and is supposed to go directly to the dishwasher and start unloading according to the schedule, and he sometimes starts looking at books instead, he is more than likely displaying childishness. He probably needs consequences, or a chore chart, etc., to turn that childishness around.

Another benchmark is the intent of the heart. Generally speaking, when a child violates a direct command or displays disrespectfulness towards a parent, it is a malicious act. The child understood what was wanted of him, but didn't care. He did not simply forget to do something or overlook something. He made a willful decision to do what he wanted to do rather than what was asked of him. When a child displays childishness, he is usually not trying to "get away with something," like in a pre-meditated instance of disobedience. This benchmark is actually the most helpful one because we can usually discern the intent of a child's heart. We know our children well, and we often know what they are thinking and what drives them.

II. CORRECTIVE CHILD TRAINING ASPECT TWO: CONSEQUENCES

A. Childishness

(1) Think as a Child

In I Corinthians, Paul says that when he was a child, he thought as a child, but now that he is grown, he thinks differently.[8] This tells us that children do not have the capability of thinking things through like adults have or should have. (The psychologist Piaget didn't have anything up on Paul!)

That's why Jacob (age seven at the time of that example) stops to watch the computer game when he is supposed to be unloading the dishes. It is why my fourteen year old son forgets to kennel the dog some nights. It is called childishness, and every child has it. (After all, in part, that's what we love about them!)

(2) Childishness Is Undeveloped Character

Childishness is really undeveloped character--that is why it needs trained through consequences instead of disciplined through spanking. While they are still children, we can train them through natural consequences to become less child-like and more character-filled. These consequences are the very things that will likely happen to them as adults if they continue those behaviors.

B. Reality Discipline

(1) Basis of Reality Discipline

I love what I learned more than twenty years ago in Kevin Leman's book, *Make Your Kids Mind Without Losing Yours*.[9] In that book, he describes reality discipline. Reality discipline says that the consequences of a child's behavior should match the behavior. We should strive to make the consequences of our children's childishness to be as natural as the consequences that an adult might encounter when he or she commits a similar infraction.

(2) It Just Makes Sense

I was a young mother, just over twenty, with only one child at the time that I read Kevin Leman's book. I remember thinking that reality discipline made so much sense. In part, I think I saw it as so appropriate because I was still an irresponsible kid myself in many ways!

Regardless of why it made sense to me, it did, and Ray and I pored over that book until we understood the concepts Mr. Leman presented. We began implementing it immediately, as much as we could. (The majority of infractions committed by a three-year-old are disobedience and require punishment.)

(3) It Is Biblical

At the time I first read *Making Children Mind Without Losing Yours,* I also happened to be reading the book of Judges in the Bible. I remember reading portions of Kevin Leman's book about a consequence matching the infraction about the same time I read about what to do if you accidentally kill your neighbor's ox: replace it. I remember meeting Ray at the door, excitedly telling him that reality discipline is biblical!

Then I continued in Judges, and time after time, God's prescription for various infractions was reality discipline. If you do this, the natural consequence will be this. If this occurs, this will happen. Not only did reality discipline make sense to me, but it also seemed to be the way God treated us much of the time.

(4) It Is What Happens in Real Life

For example, when we forget to deposit checks into our checking account, we get charged for being overdrawn (and incredibly embarrassed). When we don't clean out our junk drawer, it gets full, the drawer won't shut completely, we can't find anything, and it takes longer to clean out later when we finally get around to cleaning it. These are natural consequences.

For children, reality discipline means allowing natural consequences to have their effect or setting up consequences that are appropriate for the infraction. For our youngest, who looks at books instead of unloading the dishes after his morning routine, he might not get his computer time (his free time; he already took part of it), or he might not get to choose two stories during story time (he already looked at his books). For our older child who forgot forgetting to kennel the dog three times in a row, he, perhaps, needs more kenneling practice. Maybe he should have dog responsibility for an entire week instead of two days a week.

(5) It Requires a Balance of Grace and Justice in Implementing It

Of course, there are instances in which grace is extended. Just like the bank occasionally calls to tell us that we are overdrawn and asks us if we would like for them to move money out of the newspaper-delivery-business account into the family account, we extend grace to our irresponsible children. Just like when my husband surprises me by cleaning out the junk drawer while I'm at a meeting, thereby thwarting the natural consequences I would have endured, so I extend grace to my childish little ones.

But too much grace for my irresponsibility, and I become lax and more irresponsible. Too much grace for my seven-year-old's disregard for the dishwashing schedule, and he becomes more childish rather than less childish. Sounds like the Lord's prescription for working with us--a balance of grace and justice--grace because He loves us and justice because He loves us too much to let us remain as we are.

As parents, it is our job to help our children transition from childhood to adulthood, from childishness to responsibility. We do this by making them responsible for their behavior. We do this by giving them consequences for inappropriate irresponsibility.

Notice I say *inappropriate irresponsibility.* I always try to remember that I sometimes forget to kennel the dog when the boys are at the disability ministry and it's my responsibility. I try to remember that I sometimes do not run the dishwasher before I go to bed if the boys are gone. I try to remember that there have been times when I have had a stack of checks in my purse to deposit for days, only to discover that I forgot to deposit them, and my checking account was overdrawn. I try to remember that I sometimes let my "junk drawer" accumulate until the drawer can hardly open--and it breaks.

(6) Punishment and Consequences: No Easy Way Out

And no, none of this is easy! We had one child who, for nearly a year (between the ages of one and three), had unbearable high chair behavior. So much so that each night we had a designated "runner," someone who had to cart the little tyke upstairs to his crib when he screamed or threw his food. Every night it was a different person, so that at least some of us could enjoy the meal and interact with each other. This went on nearly every dinner for a long, long time. It was terrible. The older kids still tease the little guy about when they had to be the runner for him! However, they will not forget the endurance and determination it took to turn this behavior around--and hopefully, it will give them the motivation to persevere during difficult parenting issues themselves someday. If Ray had not been so determined, firm, and practical, I would have given up long before the results came about. I probably would have given him whatever he wanted to eat every night, just to keep peace.

Training children is a fine balance among punishment, consequences, discipling, affirmation, encouragement, and praise. It is the world's most important job--and that is not just a trite phrase for a parenting book; it truly is. We have the opportunity to help shape future adults by our faithfulness (or lack of faithfulness) to biblical child training.

"Spank, Rattle, and Roll"
Discussion/Application Questions
-- Chapter 10 --

1. If you have young children, what areas can you begin to demand first time obedience in immediately? Determine with your spouse what the discipline for disobedience will be.
2. How can you teach and instruct your children about your expectations during non-conflict times? Make a list of the times and instances in which you will discuss behavior and obedience in a non-threatening way. (Not when you are in the middle of a discipline issue.)
3. Go through various behavioral issues of your children and list whether each one is disobedience or childishness. How will you handle these differently? What punishments are appropriate for the instances of dis obedience? What consequences are appropriate for the childishness you see?
4. How can you "make the consequences fit the crime" for childish behaviors like irresponsibility, forgetfulness, procrastination, and messiness?
5. Make a commitment with your spouse to begin explaining the why's of your commands.
6. If you believe that different results require different actions, what actions can you change to get different results in your parenting?
7. Do you know the verses that deal with discipline in the Bible? If not, locate, write out, and study Scriptures on how we will discipline if we love our children, how we cannot let bad behavior continue, etc.
8. What do you place highest priority on? Character training and obedience training? Or sports, education, clubs, friends, and activities? Do you see how crucial it is in the early years to always choose training over other things?
9. What other more "modern" disciplinary techniques have you bought into? Counting to a certain number before demanding obedience? Sitting a child in time out for direct disobedience? Making a child sit in a laundry basket when he back talks? etc. What purposeful, effective techniques can replace these?

ELEVEN

It's Not All About You

Raising Children to Be Others-Focused

How can we steer children and teens away from the self-focused, number-one mentality in our world today and towards a God-honoring, servant-oriented, others-focused mentality? While we do not claim to have all of the answers, we have found some definite avenues for turning the selfishness children are born with into selflessness. Some of these answers will not surprise you--lead them into a saving knowledge of Jesus Christ, model relationship for them, and teach them to follow the Golden Rule. Others might not be what you expect--require service at home first, be faithful in small things, and teach the principle of giving according to what you have been given.

SELFLESSNESS NOT POSSIBLE WITHOUT THE SAVIOR

Ye Must Be Born Again

First of all, obviously, our children need to be born again. We, with the help of our family, friends, church body, authorities, etc., need to lead our children to a saving knowledge of Jesus Christ. Character does not last long and is not truly pure without Christ. He is the author of godly character, the giver of the fruit of the Spirit, the ultimate initiator of love, and the incarnation of all that is good.

Teach and Show the Goodness of God

As born again parents, we have to present the gospel to our children day in and day out. Yes, we must teach about the goodness of God--his love, sacrifice, and salvation, but we must also *show* the goodness of God. Quite frankly, we have to love them into God's kingdom.

Scripture tells us in I Peter 3:1 that unsaved husbands can be won through the conversation (lifestyle) of their wives: "In the same way, you wives, be submissive to your own husbands so that even if any of them are disobedient to the word, they may be won without a word by the behavior of their wives" (NASB).[1] I believe the same is true in winning our children. Our lives should show our children that we have made the decision to follow Christ---and that it was a good, no, the best, decision.

Our children should see us take joy in our salvation. They should witness first-hand the life-changing power of the cross in our lives. It should be so appealing that the thought of growing up and living without Jesus Christ seems unbearable.

Humility Is the Order of the Day

Additionally, we must show our children that we need Christ. They must understand that before we found the Savior, we were, quite honestly, lost. We were nothing without him. We had no hope of making it through this life--much less into the next one--without him.

They need to be aware that they, too, are hopeless without the miracle of salvation in their lives. Of course, it shouldn't be difficult to persuade them that life without Christ is empty and futile--just look around. When our children understand that much of the heartache in people's lives is brought on because of their separation from God, they will understand the difference that God has made in our lives compared to the hopeless lives they see in the world.

We're not suggesting that we teach our children that everything is just "hunky dory" once we're born again. But, let's face it, all of our lives would be a hundred times harder without Christ than they are with him. And our children need to understand this.

TWO PURPOSES IN LIFE

Once our children are followers of Christ, we must help them understand that there are two primary purposes,• or callings, in life:

1. To love the Lord your God with all your heart, soul, mind, and strength
2. To love your neighbor as yourself

"And you shall love the LORD your God with all your heart, and

•Obviously there are many callings on a person's life. These two are universal, biblical callings. Loving Your Neighbor as Yourself.

with all your soul, and with all your might. And the second, like it, is this: 'You shall love your neighbor as yourself.' There is no other commandment greater than these" Mark 12:30 & 31 (NKJV).[2]

Loving God

Of course, in understanding that we are to love God that deeply, we learn that we are to worship him, serve him, and do his will. And, utimately, God's will for us is to live our lives for him--serving others and bringing others into his kingdom.

We teach our children to love God more by teaching them about him. How can we (or they) not adore a God who loved us so much he died for us? How can we not be head-over-heels in love with a Savior who gave up everything for us? How can anyone not love someone who cares for us as Christ does?

Loving Your Neighbor as Yourself

Of course, we all know how to love ourselves--it is what we mere mortals do best. But God commands us to be different than the world--we are to take the love that we have for ourselves--that desire to be happy and comfortable, that urging to always be sure that we are well cared for, that intrinsic motivation to be sure that all is great in our lives--and pour that out on others instead of on ourselves. In essence, we are to be selfless--others-oriented, people-focused, and eternally minded. We are to do for others what we selfishly want to do for ourselves: "So in everything, do to others what you would have them do to you, for this sums up the Law and the Prophets" Matthew 7:12 (NIV).[3]

WITHOUT A VISION, THE PEOPLE PERISH

The Bible tells us that without a vision, people perish. "Where there is no vision, the people perish: but he that keepeth the law, happy is he" Proverbs 29:18 (KJV).[4] We have the potential, through homeschooling and the daily training of our children, to instill a vision in them. Oftentimes, we have a tendency to instill vision in our children in less-than-impacting areas. Keeping in mind that Christians are to love God with all our being and love and serve others, what kind of vision should we be instilling? Vision for Self?

Too often we are busy instilling in them a vision for success--intellectual, sports, and future career success. Too often we are busy instilling in them a vision for lifestyle--comfortable, financially profitable, and material-focused lifestyle. Too often we are busy instilling in them a vision for knowledge--high scores, excellent grades, and academic honors.

As we said earlier, there is nothing wrong with wanting good things for our children. However, while instilling in them visions for the temporal things above, we often turn their focus off of the vision God wants for them: a vision of service. It is a fine balance of helping our children discover their skills and talents preparing them for their life's work and their own future families, while still not getting so caught up in this "life." We need to help them see that while we have to have jobs, pay the bills, get an education, etc., those things should not be so consuming that we are unable to do our first two callings: love God and love others.

Vision for Service?

The Bible tells us that people perish without a vision. The same is true of children. Teenage suicide, drug use, and peer murders are all attributed to the fact that young people do not have a vision; they do not know what they are here for.

Well, we know what we're here for! The Bible is clear as to what we are to be about. And it is up to us to pass that vision on to our children.

We all understand the selflish nature of man. We all understand that children are born foolish. And we all know that selfishness and foolishness do not just go away. We must replace the vision for temporal things and self-pleasure with a vision for selflessness--a vision of a life lived for God and others.

When I Was a Child...

This turning away from selfishness and foolishness is a gradual process. It is a process that takes place over the years of childhood. Contrary to what the world teaches about normal teenhood and rebellion, the Bible makes no distinction for those years. It talks only of children gradually becoming adults.

Now I realize we do not live in "Bible culture" today, and I agree that you cannot completely separate yourself from the society in which you live. I do not think we should look and seem totally odd as we seek to "not be of the world." If no one has anything to do with us because of our strangeness, we consequently have no impact on the world around us--the very thing we are called to do.

But we do not have to accept all of the negatives that come with living in the culture. One of these negatives, in my opinion, is the "typical teen" lifestyle. We believe our teenagers can be filled with godly character and moving toward adulthood--and still be twelve to twenty years old!

I Corinthians 13:11 says, "When I was a child, I spoke as a child, I understood as a child, I thought as a child; but when I became a man, I put away childish things" I Corinthians 13:11 (NKJV).[5]

When does a child put away childishness and foolishness? As he becomes an adult--as he grows up--the very years that we have to instill in him a vision for a future life lived for God.

The word *child* in those verses denotes a *little child or minor*, but it also denotes being *unskilled or untaught*. When a person is young, he is untaught, but when he becomes an adult, he turns away from those foolish things.[6]

This turning away is described in *Strong's Concordance* as all of the following:

- causing a person or thing to have no further efficiency
- to cease
- to put an end to
- to do away with and abolish
- to be severed from or separated from

It is during the childhood years that a person is supposed to go from childishness/foolishness to adulthood. He is to sever those cords with childishness gradually as he goes from a child to an adult. In this way, childishness should begin "to have no further efficiency" for our child.

We, as parents, are given to our children to help them make this transition. It is our job to take them from the untaught, unskilled years of childhood into the years of skilled, taught adulthood. It is our job to help our children learn to follow the two greatest commandments--to love God and to love others--and it is our job to instill a vision of greatness for God within them.

BEING FAITHFUL IN SMALL THINGS FIRST

One thing that many Christian homeschooling parents do that we feel hinders selflessness training will be a shock to most parents: serving on short-term mission trips and ministry opportunities to the "uttermost parts of the earth" before serving at home. It is not the serving on a mission trip or even the peers that we see as the greatest hindrance here--it is the lack of order we follow in sending our children out.

Do the "Lesser" First, Then the "Greater"

If you have children who serve others, get along with their siblings, and love their parents, you know what an anomaly that is today. Nearly three years ago we switched churches from a small, conservative, "homeschooling" church to an extremely large, less "conservative," community-impacting church. There are nearly three thousand people in our new church. We made the switch to get back to our doctrinal roots and to allow our older teen daughters to pursue ministry degrees and ministry/leadership opportunities.

Anyway, we have met dozens and dozens of new people over the past three years, and we have come to realize how unusual the well-trained heart approach is by these encounters with unfamiliar people. All three of our daughters are active in ministry at the church, and they get asked quite frequently about their upbringing, our family, and the ministry-mindedness that our children have.

Recently, at a pastor's lunch, two of the pastors were telling Cami, who is our church's disability ministry director, that their wives had heard me speak. They were amazed at some of our teaching. One of them said, "My wife and I especially liked what your mom said about not doing school until you obey--and how she had some kids who didn't 'start school' until they were nine!"

They all laughed about this, and then Cami went on to tell them that she was never allowed to do "greater" things until the "lesser" things were done. She then related the story of when she was seven years old and wanted to help a neighbor.

The lady at the end of the lane had just had a baby and asked Cami if she wanted to come down that afternoon to help her with her new baby. Surrounded by babies and toddlers ever since they can remember, our daughters have always been crazy about them. Anyway, Cami recounted that I had told her that she could go if she got all of her chores done and finished helping with her little brothers. As the day progressed, Cami dilly dallied and did not finish her work. When it was time to go down the lane, I told her that she could not go--that there is no reason to serve others if you cannot serve your family. God wants us to first work at home, then around us, then go out to the "uttermost parts of the earth." She was heartbroken, but she worked harder on her work the next time, and was able to go eventually. Cami learned a lifelong lesson that day: serving those closest to you qualifies you to serve others.

Serving Children

Fast forward several years later when Joshua was fourteen, and we were anxious for him to "start serving." We were involved in a homeschooling ministry that had opportunities for children ages fourteen and up to minister to children with a type of Bible club, teaching all over the United States while their children's parents attended a seminar. It was well-supervised, strict, and safe, so we were anxious to get Joshua out there serving.

He went to several of these teaching opportunities. He even emptied his entire bank account of all of his hard-earned painting money one year to serve for several weeks. He did have good experiences. However, we learned a lesson through it that caused us to change our approach with our younger children: unless you are faithful in little things, you should not do "greater" things.

Joshua had always been a good kid: loving, obedient, and well-adjusted. However, when we sent him out to serve others at age fourteen, before he had, had a chance to serve "those closest" for an extended period of time, we did him a disservice. He came home, anxious to go again, anxious to serve others--but not anxious to do the “lesser” things. You see, it is always easier to serve away--the more glamorous ministry opportunities, often with friends and usually not with those who rub you the wrong way day in and day out.

You Will Be My Witnesses--Where?

I think that's why Jesus said, "But you shall receive power when the Holy Spirit has come upon you; and you shall be witnesses to Me in Jerusalem, and in all Judea and Samaria, and to the end of the earth" Acts 1:8 (NKJV).[7] That denotes an order--first closest to you, then farther from home, then all over the world--once you have shown yourself faithful to those closest.

Parents often send their children on mission trips in the hopes that they (1) will learn to serve others; and (2) will develop a taste for missions or ministry of some kind. Yet, we feel strongly that if a child cannot serve those closest to him, day in and day out, then he has no business serving those abroad. If he does not cheerfully serve the family by doing the dishes, why should he go build a bridge for others? What has qualified him for that “greater” work?

Serve Your Family, Then Serve Others

We followed a different protocol for our girls, who were next in line by age. While Joshua has turned out great, we still feel strongly that the method we used with the girls regarding service is superior. They have all been taught that if you are not faithful in serving at home, you are not qualified to serve outside of the home.

Once each of our two older daughters was found faithful in the daily ins and and outs of serving at home, then she has broadened her serving--though still from home and usually with her parents or siblings. Our daughters have gone from dish washing and laundry at home, to doing newsletter writing and debate tournament preparation. Then, once they were faithful in those services near home, they have gone from then to serving locally: helping with area homeschooling events, teaching and leading young teen girls clubs, scrubbing mattresses at the homeless shelter, reading to and playing piano for elderly at nursing homes, and serving in disability ministry. From there, once found faithful, they have moved on to leadership in local church ministries--Cami leading disability ministry and Kayla leading and teaching young adults. From there, they have traveled stateside to serve in disaster relief, at Joni and Friends family retreats, and at conferences. They each took their first overseas mission trip during their sophomore years of college.

Our next two children, Kara and Jonathan, have followed similar paths. They served the family through cleaning and laundry (among many other tasks) then served homeschoolers through our ministry, working for our publishing company, and helping Mom and Dad with speech and debate. As they have shown themselves faithful in those, they have branched out to serve at church in disability ministry without Mom and Dad and in physical labor like moving, cleaning, etc. at church. Last summer, when

Kara turned seventeen, she took two "stateside" ministry trips--one with the Academy of Arts' (A of A) Jamestown quasintennial project/drama and the other with the A of A's summer traveling drama program, ministering the message of chastity and pro-life through drama in the southern United States. Jonathan desires to serve with the Academy of Arts, and he knows the unwritten list of requirements and home-grown service opportunities he has to meet before we will even consider his traveling to serve.

There are many patterns and orders in Scripture. If we look at these more closely, we would probably see there is a reason and wisdom for them. Good things happen when we put things in their proper order--and the same is true in the training of our children.

To Whom Much Is Given

Upon Kayla's high school graduation, her life verse was "To whom much is given, much is expected." As Christians, we all have the responsibility to use that which was given to us. There are many ways to teach this to our children. The Bible is full of stories and parables relating this theme. The story of the talents is a perfect example of this teaching that children can relate to. Jesus' words to not "hide our light under a bushel" further expounds on this principle.

We need continual teaching and awareness in our homes that this life is not our own; we were bought with a price. That we are here for great things. That we are not to waste that which was given to us. That we are to give away what we have been given--and then God will multiply it many times over. That "to whom much is given, much is expected." These are the things of the heart--these are the things that cause us (and will cause our children) to be others-focused.

In Kayla's high school graduation speech, she reiterated the impact that this teaching had, had on her life: "Ever since I was little, my parents told me that I was here for great things. That my life was not my own. And, that when you are given a lot, a lot is expected of you. I knew at a young age that I was given a lot--and that because I was given a lot, a lot would be expected."

When we, and our children, understand that "it's not about us," we will be ready to focus on others. We will be eager to give that which was given to us. We will be prepared to do great things for God and others.

"It's Not All About You"
Discussion/Application Questions
-- Chapter 11 --

1. How can you change your lifestyle to win your children to the Lord? Not just outward things, like avoiding things you do not think you should read or see, but also in the way you relate to them (with more gentleness, kindness, and empathy) and the joy you exhibit in your salvation?
2. Do your children sense that you are utterly helpless without the Lord? Do you portray a certain level of "self-madeness" that makes them feel that the Lord is simply "fire insurance" in your life and that you could make it without him?
3. Do you focus your teaching with your children on the fact that the two greatest commands Christ gave us are to love the Lord and love others?
4. What kind of vision do you predominately instill in your children? Do your children feel that you desire them to live for Christ and others more than you desire their temporal success?
5. Do you see the childhood years as a gradual turning away from childishness to responsibility and adulthood or do you treat your children as though they are children until some magical time when they become adults?
6. How can you instill in your youngest children the idea that you should do lesser things first in order to qualify yourself for greater things?
7. Do you agree that when you send your children out to serve before they have served closer to home, you are potentially thwarting the way God sends us out?
8. Have you seen an attitude in your children in which they want to serve others, take missions trips, and do things at church but they do not desire to serve at home?

TWELVE

So How Do You Really Feel About That?

Teaching Children Empathy

If I could only instill one character quality in my children out of all of the dozens of qualities they could acquire, it would be empathy. You see, once a child has empathy, he has a much higher likelihood of utilizing all of the other character qualities we desire for him to have. Sure, a child can be diligent, but without empathy causing him to feel that someone needs something done, diligence might not help him much. A person can be extremely kind, but without the ability to see others' needs and extend that kindness, that quality can literally go unused. A Christian may be as loving as can be, but without the ability to see the unlovely ones, that love will not be spread as high and as wide and as deep as it could be.

Empathy may be defined as *a consistent consciousness of others. An awareness of others' needs with the desire to meet those needs. Walking in another's shoes--and a deep longing to act upon the knowledge gained from walking in those shoes.* Or, simply *seeing others' needs and truly wanting to meet them.*

In Harper Lee's novel, *To Kill a Mockingbird*, Scout's father, Atticus Finch, teaches his young daughter about empathy after she had a confrontation with her teacher. He says it in such a way that one cannot help understand the very heart of empathy training, that of getting into someone's skin and seeing life from his perspective: "'...if you can learn a simple trick, Scout, you'll get along a lot better with all kinds of folks. You never really understand a person until you consider things from his point of view--until you climb into his skin and walk around in it.'"[1] That is truly the depth of empathy training our children need.

EMPATHY SHOULD BEGIN AT HOME

Not All About You

As the previous chapter's title declares, a major aspect of teaching children to be others-minded is instilling in them this true fact: *it's not all about you*. In our self-absorbed society, this is harder to do than ever. We have lost our basic consideration of others. A friend recently told me, "There are only three people in my life who ever ask me anything about me. Everyone else always talks about herself." Sad, but true.

In child-controlled homes, the children are often set up to think that everything actually is about them. After all, they whimper, fuss, roll their eyes, or throw a fit, and things around them change.

The world must revolve around them with that kind of power at their disposal.

The initial way to stop this, as suggested earlier, is to avoid or dismantle that child-controlled home and put the family members in their proper places. But even if we do instill proper, biblical child-training from babyhood, a part of that foolishness may still remain. The monster of selfishness continues to rear its ugly head.

This is where a change of mind--a different way of thinking, and acting, and talking--comes into play. From our children's earliest years, we have told them that it is not all about them. Oh, we love them, affirm them, encourage them, play with them, train them, give good gifts to them, and many other loving parental acts. I adore my children! But the world does not revolve around them, and until they understand that other people are more important than they are, they will never fully be able to live a God-first, people-second life--for they will always put themselves in that first place slot.

Prefer Others

One of Joshua's first memory verses when he could barely talk was Romans 12:10--"In love of the brethren be tenderly affectioned one to another; in honor *preferring one another*" Romans 12:10 (ASV).[2] I can still remember him as a toddler saying... "'fer others 'fore self" (prefer others before yourself).

A recurring command in our home is not so much "obey," as much as "prefer." When one child complains about being mistreated by another, we question the offender with, "Are you preferring?" When one child is singled out for consistently wanting the best, we ask, "Are you preferring others before yourself?" And even when the children have tattled through the years, they would often say, "So and so's not preferring!"

From young ages, each child was instructed to leave the best and biggest for someone else. To give the "choice" seat to another. To yield his rights and desires for the best to someone else. To defer his wants to a brother or sister. Obviously, our children didn't always follow these instructions (after all they were children!). However, these principles were consistently taught and re-taught, explained and re-explained. And, little by little, we saw this teaching come to fruition in our home more often than not.

Early on, we made it clear that we were not here on this earth for ourselves; we were here for the Lord and others. Putting ourselves behind others is what we are supposed to be characterized by, and all the more in our own homes.

I'm Number Three

We have a mantra with our little guys to remind them of the concept of putting others before themselves: "You're number three." We have explained to them that God should be first, others second, and we should be number three. Sometimes all we have to do is hold up three fingers during a dispute between two of them, and they remember--"Oh, yeah, I should put him before myself. I'm third."

Other times it takes much more than the "three symbol" to remind our children of where they should stand with others. Many times it has not been simply "Prefer" or "Three." It has taken long nights of discussing how God sees things. It has taken rivers of tears and avalanches of prayers in order to help our children see how God wants us to live in our relationships. Whether it is as simple as making a "three" sign or as extensive as a week without sleep, teaching our children the important order of God's kingdom is worth it.

To Be Great in God's Kingdom, Be the Servant of All

Now, you might wonder if all of our emphasis on putting self behind others, putting others first, thinking more of others than we do ourselves, etc., has hurt anyone's psyche in our home. Rest assured, it hasn't. You see, we are bombarded daily with the message that we are the important ones, that we have to watch out for ourselves because no one else will. The danger is simply not there of our developing "inferiority complexes" or "poor self esteem" through putting others first.

Besides, Scripture makes it crystal clear that if you want to truly be great, you should serve others: "Sitting down, Jesus called the Twelve and said, 'If anyone wants to be first, he must be the very last, and the servant of all'" Mark 9:35 (NIV).[3] Putting others first is the way to true greatness.

How Does That Make Him Feel?

Next to "prefer" (and more recently, "three"), our second most common mantra through the years has probably been, "How does that make him feel?" You see, while we did not want our children to get hung up on themselves all the time--always concerned that they were getting shorted, that they were not getting the best, that they were being mistreated--we *did* want them to get hung up on how other people felt. We can hurt others, damage relationships, and cause someone to stumble without even realizing we are doing so. Helping our children see how our actions make others feel is one of the best gifts we can give to them in living for Christ, not to mention the incredible impact it can make on their future marriages!

Reading Faces

Because we are basically self-absorbed people, we often miss the cues of others' pain. We literally trained our children to read people's faces, look into their hearts, and even discern body language to determine how others feel. Some of our children learned this more easily than others; a couple of them were practically born counselors, it seemed. They took to our cues immediately and would often tell us how people around us felt. Whether we were in museums, Grandma's house, church, or the grocery, our little empathizers would point out someone and say, "Look, Mommy, that person looks like he is having a hard time." Or "Did you see how his shoulders were slumped? He looked so sad."

They also learned how to read each other. Again, some better than others, but they were at least all made aware of it over and over again. One would say, "Did you see how Kara looked? I could tell you hurt her feelings." Or, "Did you see the look on Jonathan's face? He was trying to be a good sport, but I could tell he was hurt. We need to be extra careful to encourage him, since he didn't place in his speech, and he feels really disappointed."

Appearance Is Reality

Then we took our empathy training one step further. Ray brought business principles home and applied them to the kids' relationships with each other and with us. Our new slogan became "Appearance is reality!" In summary, we taught the children that even if you didn't mean to do it, didn't think you did it, or truly didn't do it, if the other person felt like you did--to that person, you did it.

Many a night we were up late, talking with a young teen about his or her behavior toward a sibling.

> Young teen: But I didn't do that. She is just making that up.
>
> Mom and Dad: But she felt like you did.
>
> Young teen: That's because she's such a baby. I didn't do anything to her. She's just a wimpy sandwich.•
>
> Mom and Dad: It doesn't matter if she is a wimpy sandwich. She feels that you did it; she is hurt; and it is your responsibility to do something about it.
>
> Young teen: Why do I have to do something about it when it's all in her head?
>
> Mom and Dad: Because you are responsible for how you made her feel. If there wasn't at least a little truth in it, she wouldn't feel that way. Did you think it, even if you didn't do it?
>
> Young teen: I might have thought it, but that's not the point. The point is, I didn't do it.
>
> Mom and Dad: The point isn't whether you did it or not. The point is that it appears to her that you did it--and appearance is reality.

•A wimpy sandwich is a type of sloppy joe that our school caferteria used to serve when Ray and I were in high school; it has become a negative term used in our home when someone was being a "baby." Somehow it has stuck through the years--guess they had to learn it from Mom and Dad, huh?

Obviously, this can be taken to an extreme in which the one being offended is ultra-sensitive and over-consumed with his own feelings all of the time--being victimized when it simply isn't true. Our goal in this training was not to make the one being hurt feel justified, but rather to make each of our children realize that any part of someone's hurt that you are involved in is your responsibility--and that every action, word, or deed has the potential to hurt others.

If Your Brother Has Aught Against You

This concept actually originated in the Bible. (Not too shocking, huh?) Many relational concepts that do not flow with our "natural reaction" originated in the Bible!) In Jesus' Sermon on the Mount, he practically says the same thing: if your brother thinks you did something to him, and he is mad at you--go to him and make it right: "Moreover if your brother sins against you, go and tell him his fault between you and him alone. If he hears you, you have gained your brother" Matthew 18:15 (NKJV).[4] Do this before you do anything else--because appearance is reality.

You see, we can't make something right if we constantly justify our behavior. We can't ask forgiveness if we feel that the person is just being ultra-sensitive and practically making it all up anyway. We can only ask forgiveness if we are selfless enough to see that it doesn't matter what the other person does or says--our part in any disagreement is wrong and needs to be corrected.

EXPLAIN EVERYTHING

They Do Not Know If We Do Not *Tell* Them

Now obviously, we didn't just make everyone apologize and go on. But it was a beginning to our children's understanding that any part you play in a broken relationship is your responsibility--and any part that someone thinks you played is also your responsibility. Selfishness makes us want to show others our rightness and their wrongness. Selflessness makes us think (and say), *I don't care if I was right or wrong. It doesn't matter. All that matters is that relationship is restored, because that is what Jesus would do.*

In getting our children to the point that they saw that appearance is reality, we learned to explain everything (again!). We frequently explained the process that the other person went through to become hurt. Remember, we had three girls in a row--that made for a lot of hurt feelings and misunderstandings--and opportunities to teach proper responses to those misunderstandings! Explain what someone thinks and feels when someone does this or says that. Explain irrational and rational thinking, and our responses to both of them.

They Do Not Know If We Do Not *Show* Them

Not only did we explain everything to them about relationships, constantly, but we also explained everything to them about everything--literally. Again, we are not programmed to be selfless. We are not programmed to automatically think about others. We are born with a sin nature--a selfish nature. We need someone to explain to us how bad that sin nature is, how to get rid of it (or at least how to live above it through Christ), and how to live a life that is pleasing to God.

I remember a trip we took to Chicago many years ago, when the older children were ten through fourteen. We spent a long weekend visiting museums, swimming at our motel, and, of course, talking. We had many opportunities to see those with needs and discuss these situations. Before we left that weekend, we had written a song (amateur poet/songwriter here) that described what we saw and felt that we still sing today:

> I prayed for you today, though I didn't know your name,
> I saw a hurting look, so I had to stop and pray.
> I prayed for you today, when I saw you on the street,
> Playing on your trumpet, for everyone you meet.
>
> (Chorus) I know it doesn't seem like much, just a simple little prayer.
> But I want you to realize there is a God who cares.
> I know it doesn't seem like much, I wish I could do more.
> But the very best thing that I can do is take you to the Lord.
>
> I prayed for you today, when I saw you with your cane,
> Your yesterdays have flown right by, and now you're old and lame.
> I prayed for you today, when I saw you on your porch,
> You looked so sad and lonely, so broken and forlorn.
>
> (Chorus) I know it doesn't seem like much, just a simple little prayer.
> But I want you to realize there is a God who cares.
> I know it doesn't seem like much, I wish I could do more.
> But the very best thing that I can do is take you to the Lord.
>
> I prayed for you today, when I saw you with your friends,
> Trying to be popular, trying to fit in.
> I prayed for you today, when I saw you at the zoo,
> Being a daddy all alone is difficult to do.
>
> (Chorus) I know it doesn't seem like much, just a simple little prayer.
> But I want you to realize there is a God who cares.
> I know it doesn't seem like much, I wish I could do more.
> But the very best thing that I can do is take you to the Lord.

Before You, After You, and Beside You

In their popular *Growing Kids God's Way* parenting series,[5] Gary and Anne Marie Ezzo teach an anti-selfishness concept that we also implemented with our children--that of constantly thinking of *the people before you, the people after you, and the people beside you.* This paradigm helped us instill in our children the idea that you are not an island; everything you do and say affects those around you. What is the impact of what you are doing on those who have gone before you (consistency in your family, honoring your grandparents, fulfilling what was begun for you, etc.)? What about those beside you (those you are in relationship with right at this moment)? And what about those following you--those who will come after you (in leaving messes behind, in doing anything to help lighten the load of the next person, in being a good example to those who are younger or weaker, etc.)?

This practice, combined with explaining everything, has been the basis for much of our selflessness training. Keeping our children and ourselves ever mindful of others in all situations is what the before you, beside you, after you training is all about.

Now, I have to admit that this has been easier for us than it is for some because of who I am married to! Ray is the epitome of selflessness. If the Bible didn't make it clear that we are all born selfish, I would think the man was born selfless. He is literally what qualifies us to write this book. He is the originator of the well-trained heart approach.

The children love to hear the story of when Daddy was in junior high and a poor boy starting coming to school with mismatched and old clothing. Ray started wearing mismatched and old clothing to make the boy comfortable--and he had not even heard the born-again message at that time. (I tell the kids that's why Daddy can't match clothes to this very day!) Ray has been the "poster dad" for the before you, beside you, and after you concept. And our children want to be just like him.

But junior high sweetness aside, we can all instill this teaching in our children--if we are willing to go to the" Savior's School of Selflessness" ourselves. This is where it gets tricky, once again. But, as in all child training, when we truly accept the fact that we cannot give our children anything we ourselves do not have, we get a little more serious about our own shortcomings.

No, Ray is not perfect. We do not have to be perfect to teach our children selflessness and how to live for Christ. We just have to be making a genuine attempt to do so ourselves. That's what our children really require--that we are honestly trying to live what we are teaching them.

Remember that transparency we referred to in "Let It Begin With Me"? Our transparency is another teaching aid. We explain that we didn't mean to be that way, that we don't want to be that way, that we, too, are in the "Savior's School of Selflessness." We truly never graduate from this school, but we can keep moving towards the final goal--living a life that pleases God and serves others.

Moral Banks and Learning Hooks

Let's go back to the discussion of explaining everything. The Ezzo's and Gregg Harris[6] teach this in their seminars, as do Dr. Tim Kimmel[7] and Kevin Leman[8] in their books. It is exceptional parenting--and the vehicle by which our children best learn about life.

The Ezzo's describe the idea of explaining everything to our children as filling up their "moral banks." We fill our child's moral banks with the how's of living--of relationships, character lessons, godliness, etc. Then, when he is in a similar situation down the road, he can go to that moral bank and make a withdrawal, that is, draw out the deposit that you previously made in his bank and use that deposit to determine his behavior in the current situation.

Ray and I call these explanations of everything (including academic instruction) "learning hooks." When we teach or explain something to our child, he has a hook with that topic in it within him. Then when he encounters a situation in which that hook would apply, he simply hooks the situation right onto that previously created hook. He has "learning hooks" to hook new information onto--to create groupings, if you will, of information and situations for future learning and behaviors.

For example, Jacob, our youngest, went through a time when he did not play well with his two older brothers. He has had a difficult time learning the process of selflessness, though he is sweet and humble and truly wants to learn. Anyway, I told him over and over again, "If you don't learn to be more selfless and yield your rights to have things your way when you play, someday nobody will want to play with you." In terms of reality discipline, the reality of the situation is that if you are not nice, nobody likes you. Period. Adult or child.

One day Jacob came to me in tears, just sobbing his little heart out: "Mommy, it's just like you said. You were right. Nobody will want to be my friend if I am selfish. I just asked Josiah if he wanted to go upstairs and play Legoes with me, and he said, no because I always have to have my own way. Even my own brother doesn't want to play with me because I am selfish."

Jacob had a learning hook created for him: if you are selfish, nobody will want to be around you. When he came into a new situation that he did not know how to handle, he could turn to that hook and hook this new experience right onto it. It was already built there for him to associate a similar situation or outcome with.

We have spent our children's years at home creating learning hooks for them, teaching them what the Bible says, what the world is like, what people think and feel, and what our response to people and situations should be. They each have literally hundreds of hooks to "hook" new situations and experiences onto. And those hooks help them determine their responses to those new situations and experiences.

END GOAL OF EMPATHY TRAINING: DO GOOD

Do Good When It Is in Your Power to Do It

The Ezzo's have taken a lot of grief for what has been termed as their "shopping cart teaching." In this teaching, the Ezzo's explain to parents that in order to teach their children to consider those before them, beside them, and after them, they must do so themselves--beginning with returning shopping carts to the cart corrals rather than leaving them in the parking lot to scratch up others' cars, make more work for their gatherers, and take up parking spaces.

I have heard many Ezzo students say that this is craziness: What difference does it make what I do with my shopping cart? I'm busy. It's not my fault the cart corral is so far away. I can't help it if people park too close to my abandoned cart, etc. etc.

In reality, these parents do not want to take the hard classes in the "Savior's School of Selflessness"--and their children will never want to either. What's the big deal? It's just a shopping cart?

It's not that it is a shopping cart. It is that we know someone needs something (cart available, cart not loose, etc.), and it is within our power to do something about it, but we do not. We are lazy, apathetic, and selfish. Rather than take thirty extra seconds to lighten someone else's load, we choose to keep those thirty seconds for ourselves and increase someone else's load.

So what do we do once we see others' hurts and needs? What is the end goal of empathy training? The end goal of empathy training is the following: that our children will be skilled and trained enough in their areas of ministry and various areas of life that when they do feel empathetic and see needs, they will do what they can to meet them. *They will do good when it is in their power to do so.*

See a Need, Meet a Need

Our family has been given skills of organization, efficiency, leadership, and diligence. We have been trained in cooking; cleaning; office skills; computer skills; writing (creating computer-generated charts, cards, posters, notices, newsletters, etc.); acting, speaking, and drama; studying; teaching; and much more. Different family members are stronger in some areas than others, but each one of us has very definite, useful, potentially helpful skills. All families do. One of the things we have taught our children from very early in their lives is the verse that explains, "Do not withhold good from those to whom it is due, When it is in the power of your hand to do so" Proverbs 3:27 (NKJV).[9]

We have coupled empathy training with action--if you have the ability, time, money, tools, etc., to meet a need you see, try to meet it. This must be tempered with prioritizing and working in the ministries you are called to, but it is a good rule of thumb to live by in serving Christ.

For us, this has translated into taking on jobs and tasks individually, and as a family, that are in our skill areas. It might mean going that extra mile, sleeping less, working more---but, if you can handle it, you should do it.

This is actually how our family began writing homeschooling curriculum. When my older children were little, they would come to the table each day with their arms full of language arts books---grammar, composition, creative writing, vocabulary, daily English drills, penmanship, spelling, etc. I always thought it would be nice to have all of those books in one book---and have it be based on worthwhile text, too. Of course, at that time, I couldn't do anything about that desire; I did not have the ability or time to meet that need.

However, several years later, when we were no longer having babies, we kept being reminded of teaching we had heard from Bill Gothard[10] and Gregg Harris: when you see a need that you can meet, meet it. (They both taught this from the standpoint of ministry as well as from the perspective of potential home industries and business ventures.) So, we began writing curriculum as a ministry for the Advanced Training Institute, to try to lighten the loads of the moms in their program who had many children to teach. From that has grown our own curriculum development and publishing company, which, in turn, is funding our speaking, writing, and counseling ministry to homeschoolers---all because we saw a need, had the ability to meet it, and did so.

If You Can Handle It, Do It

Early on in our Christian life we had a tendency to be judgmental and, therefore, ineffective for Christ. We judged non-Christians and kept our children away from them, rather than doing good to them and loving them. Now, there is a fine balance to this. I do not believe in putting your children in dangerous situations. However, we took this to an extreme--judging our non-Christian relatives, not wanting our children to be around them because they smoked or used offensive language, etc.

In the process of this, we turned our relatives off. They did not see the good training we were doing with our children; they just saw how we didn't want to come to extended family gatherings for fear they would influence our children with their Marlboros. They knew they were being judged, and they didn't appreciate it.

We saw the ineffectiveness of this (and the wrongness of it) and set about to change it. Rather than not attending gatherings or keeping our children far away from others' cigarettes and television, we began reaching out to them. We didn't preach to them; we didn't wear sandwich boards telling of their impending doom to the get-togethers. We simply began doing good to them.

We told the children that we have the ability, money, and tools to make good food to take to the gatherings. We have the manpower to help clean up. We have the fun-mindedness to bring games, lively Christmas music, and children's videos. And we did.

It wasn't long before our relatives looked forward to our coming. It became "the Reishes are here," rather than "the party-poopers are here." We would spend an hour together on the morning of an event, peeling twenty pounds of potatoes, while listening to talking books and having a blast, fixing the creamiest, yummiest mashed potatoes ever. We baked for weeks before an event and took huge trays of delicious goodies. We would head up euchre tournaments, ping-pong rounds, and fun table games. We stayed afterwards and did dishes and put the rooms back together.

No longer did people dread our coming. We were doing good to others--and people like to have good done to them. They came to respect us and our way of life. They often ask about our children and our training. They are impressed with the kindness, helpfulness, goodness, and diligence of our children. Our kids learned that when you do good to others, it is like doing good for Jesus: "Or when did we see You sick, or in prison, and come to You? And the king will answer and say to them, 'Assuredly, I say to you, inasmuch as you did it to one of the least of these My brethren, you did it to Me'" Matthew 25: 39-40 (NKJV).[11] And, they learned that when it is within your power to do good, you should do it.

Of course, we benefit from this way of living too. It is a joy to get together with relatives and just be who were are, without judging and without facades. It is relaxing and rejuvenating to play games, laugh, and share a meal without the pressures we had when we were constantly looking at negatives.

People Should Want to Have You Around

Yes, people should want to have us around. We should be energy-givers, energizing and encouraging others. They should not dread our arrival as the judgmental, holier-than-thou families living this weird homeschooling life. Nor should they dread the arrival of our children! Now, obviously, this does not happen overnight, but we have found that if you live an others-oriented life, giving instead of taking, and loving instead of judging, others will desire to have you around.

Twenty years ago we were out of place in many situations. We didn't have much to say to non-Christians. We didn't want to take the time for our relatives. We had so many other things important things to do. We thought that by being different, we were somehow witnessing for Christ.

Now, after changing this lack in our lives, we can go to ballroom dances, sit down with people who never go to church, ask about their lives, encourage them in their relationships and jobs, answer questions about our family and homeschooling, and come away earning the respect of people, rather than turning them off so badly that they would never want the faith we have anyway.

As a side note, Ray and I were just blessed by our ballroom dance studio with the high honor of "students of the year." This award was given for "encouraging other students and supporting the studio." We received a lovely plaque and affirmation from our teacher and others in the studio. Prior to receiving this award, we did not even know it existed. (We had not been able to attend the annual ball in which it is presented during the previous two years of our dancing there.) We were not in this to receive acclaim. We were just doing what God has shown us over the past several years (and what we have taught our children): doing good to those around us.

I cringe when I hear homeschoolers go on and on about how nobody at church likes them, their parents disagree with their homeschooling, and people at work think they're strange. I understand that some grandparents, no matter how hard you try, cannot be reasoned with. And I know that many folks at church are opposed to homeschooling regardless of what we do to positively influence them. However, some homeschoolers seem to wear these attributes as badges of honor, feeling that they are following Jesus' teaching about "leaving your mother and father" and "the world hating you" in order to live the gospel in their homes.

We feel homeschoolers who do this are missing some extremely crucial teachings in that whole process: do good when it is in your power; when you do something unto the least of these, you are doing it to Christ; live a life blameless and upright, so that nobody has anything to say against the gospel; honor your parents; to name a few.

In the beginning, like many other homeschoolers' extended families, our parents questioned our homeschooling. They especially questioned the areas that we judged them in. However, they have changed their minds. As we have faithfully applied the concept of doing good to them, they have seen the fruits in our children---who also do good to them, love them, respect them, and reach out to them. They love homeschooling now---or as they tell us, they love the way we homeschool! How could people whose grandchildren are loving, kind, serving, communicative, and respectful not approve of the method by which their grandchildren become those types of people?

Acting on the Before You, Beside You, and After You Paradigm

Let's review again the others-thinking and explaining everything principles. Our children always knew that they could choose others or themselves; in nearly every situation we have those choices. They knew because we taught them others-thinking and, need I repeat it, we explained everything to them.

Many parents say things like, "Stop the attitude," or, "Change that face." But attitudes and faces are simply reflections of the heart. Rather than yelling out what external factors we want changed, we need to explain to them why they are doing what they are doing. We must explain the effect that that behavior has on others and God's view of it.

The same is true of others-thinking. There is hardly a day (or hour!) that goes by that we do not explain something to our children about others: "See kids, I'm pulling all the way up against the car in front of me, so someone can park behind me, and not have to parallel park." To, "Wipe that pop off the table, so someone else can use this table right away when we leave." To, "When there are not enough seats for everyone, Reishes always 'pick up some floor'" (our family instruction for giving someone else your seat).

We have the opportunity! We can do this! We can teach our children a way of life far greater than any other. We have it within our power "to do good to others." We just have to rise to the challenge.

Empathy Training Full Circle

Let me leave you with a final example of our empathy and selflessness training that came full circle nine years ago, benefiting me, and eventually thousands of others in the Advanced Training Institute. I was pregnant with our eighth baby, who would die in a few months during an intra-uterine blood transfusion. I was sick emotionally and physically. I had seven children, fourteen and under, including a needy toddler that required a lot of training and patience. Ray worked sixty to eighty hours a week. Add to all of this a high-risk pregnancy. I was struggling during that season of my life probably more than any other.

It was at that time that Ray questioned Kayla, age thirteen at the time, about ministry. He asked her who she was going to minister to. Kayla responded by saying that she was going to be a missionary to Central or South America. Ray questioned her further: "No, I mean now. Who are you going to minister to right now in your life?"

Kayla thought for a quick moment, looked up at Ray and said, "Right now, my ministry will be Mom."

Kayla had been trained since she was a little girl that she had a higher purpose on this earth, that she had abilities, talents, skills, character, and training to do great things for God. She had been trained in empathy--watch out for others, do good, serve people, love God. And I was to become the recipient of the fruit of her training.

At age thirteen, Kayla immediately stepped up her work. She had already been the most diligent child I had ever seen, but now she pressed in even harder. She would get up early, before anyone else was up, work in the kitchen, do dishes, fix breakfast. I would doze in and out of a nauseated, worried sleep to hear her banging around in the kitchen--ministering to me.

She never tired of it. She took on more and more work, even helping the other kids with their chores, so I wouldn't have to worry about things getting done. After our stillbirth and the loss of our fertility, I began a writing ministry for ATI, and she continued serving the family, taking care of the kitchen, freezers, meals, and food storage almost single-handedly.

Before she knew it, she found that after doing the "lesser" things for two years, she, too, was writing curriculum, serving thousands of children all around the US and the world, providing at-cost language arts curriculum for them, without expecting or receiving anything in return. And all because she chose Mom as her ministry. All because she *did good to others when it was in her power to do it.*

"So How Do You Really Feel About That?" Discussion/Application Questions -- Chapter 12 --

1. What do you see as the most vital character quality to instill in your children and why?
2. If you have young children, how can you instill in them the idea of preferring others before themselves?
3. Instead of shouting out to your children that they should stop it and be nice, how can you become a "how does that make you feel" parent to your children?
4. Do you yourself feel that appearance is reality or do you find yourself justifying your behavior towards someone, saying that it was misunderstood, not your fault, etc? Can you get to the place in your own life where you can say, "It doesn't matter if it is my fault or not."
5. Do you explain things clearly to your children? If you are not in the habit of explaining relational issues to your children, start keeping a tally on a sticky note or somewhere of each time you take that extra step or go that extra mile to explain something about relationships to them. (You will probably find that as you begin explaining things, they will start asking you more and more-and help you remember to do so!)
6. Do you see a need in your family to use the "before you, beside you, and after you" model of selflessness training? How can you begin?
7. Have you been the kind of parent who didn't explain why something should be done because "you are the parent, and kids should listen to you"? If so, how do you feel about explaining things in order to give your children learning hooks on which to hook future experiences?
8. Do you return your shopping cart? :
9. What skills, talents, abilities, and resources does your family have to invest in others? Have a family meeting and discuss this-and deter mine one thing you will do together with what you have been given.
10. Do people dread having your children around? Be honest. You can tell this a mile away if it is true. How can you turn this around?

THIRTEEN

The Socialization Traps

Socialization and the Well-Trained Heart

Over a dozen years ago, homeschooling father, Rick Boyer, wrote a compelling book entitled *The Socialization Trap.*[1] Its premise was that homeschoolers were getting caught up in the idea that children who were taught at home were unsocialized and needed similar socialization as children in school. He recommended that we avoid the socialization trap of much peer interaction and instead protect our children from negative influences. I devoured this book from cover to cover several times and gleaned much from it.

Many of its points were true, and continue to be so as evidenced by the fact that when asked about socialization, the first response from many homeschooling parents is something like the following: "Oh, we take part in so many activities that socialization is not a problem."

In this, we are asserting that, *no, you don't have to worry about us as we are providing the same socialization opportunities as school children have.* We are, in essence, saying that whatever home-schooling causes us to lack in socialization, we are making up for with myriad activities, just like schools have. Ultimately, we are admitting that yes, people are right, homeschooling does not provide proper socialization, so we are compensating for it by adopting the schools' methods--more activities, sports, youth groups, clubs, and other opportunities for children to be with other children--the appropriate model for socialization.

WHAT ARE THE SOCIALIZATION TRAP**S**?

Two Traps

After reading *The Socialization Trap* and observing families who adopt a more isolated approach to socialization, we have found that extreme isolationism often produces protected children, but not necessarily well-socialized children. Likewise, we have seen much negative fruit in the opposite approach to socialization---that of trying to "do it just like schools do."

Over the course of homeschooling for nearly two dozen years, we have discovered many approaches to socialization that do and do not work. From these, we have decided that in reality there is not a socialization *trap* (of trying to socialize our children like schools do as Boyer's book points out), but rather there are socialization *traps*--two traps that homeschoolers tend to fall in--one on each end of the spectrum, neither of which results in properly socialized children when strictly adhered to.

Defining "Proper Socialization"

Before revealing what we see as the two socialization traps (and offering our solutions for some of the socialization problems), we must define "proper socialization." I think a lot of issues with socialization could be avoided if parents would decide ahead of time what they see as appropriate socialization--and what they want their children's socialization to look like in the end. Again, it is about planning ahead of time (prioritizing) what your family life will be.

A year or so ago Kayla developed a workshop for homeschooling parents about socialization. It is extremely insightful, especially so since it comes from a young person who was homeschooled her entire life. Of special interest to me was her definition of proper socialization. She so eloquently put into words what Ray and I have always felt that proper socialization of our children should look like.

Her definition went as follows: "Protecting children from the world for a short time so they can be witnesses to the world for a lifetime."

With that as our premise, we can examine the two socialization traps that homeschoolers often fall into more discernibly, and determine what our socialization approach will be.

EXTREME 1: ISOLATION

Parent With Wisdom, Not With Fear

I remember that when Joshua was little, we would not allow the word Santa Claus to be used in our home. We would not allow

Joshua to see Santa's in books, posters, on the street, etc. If he ever did accidentally view a Santa, we told Joshua that, that man was evil. Anyway, one time he saw Santa in a grocery, and not knowing what or who he was, Joshua exclaimed, "Look Mommy, it's Moses."

That was a humorous moment--one that our entire family loves to tell. But, how much better would it have been for Joshua to have known about the original Santa--a saint who did good for others. How much better would it have been for us to explain to Joshua that, that man's goodness was over-emphasized to the point that people made a sort of god out of him through the years (after his death)--making him omnipotent, omniscient, replacing the true God. How much better would it have been for us to explain to Joshua that when we focus on Santa Claus, it takes away from the true meaning of Christmas--and what Jesus did for us. But instead, we parented in fear...fear of Santa Claus.

Now, through our debate training and through a more in-depth look at the Scriptures, we parent less in fear and more in wisdom. Oh, I still have fearful moments. There are some areas in which no amount of wisdom can seem to overcome my fears--especially when it comes to my older children's future spouses! But parenting in wisdom--being wary of dangers, explaining and teaching about those dangers, and giving heart training concerning those dangers--has resulted in more lasting commitments for our children than the simple, "Don't look at Santa; he's evil."

This first socialization model is similar to our Santa example. It is based on fear--fear that somebody will influence our child in a negative way and lead him away from us and away from the Lord. In this extreme, we are aware of the dangers--other children's attitudes and behaviors, non-Christians' ungodly actions, and the immoral world in general--and think that if we keep our children far away from all of it until they are grown, they will be Christians when they are adults.

There is a lot of truth to fearing others' negative influences in our children's lives. After all, the Bible says that foolishness is bound in the heart of a child, and it is the parents' responsibility to remove it.[2] How can we remove it if we constantly put them with other children who are also filled with foolishness? According to the Bible, bad companions corrupt people: "Do not be deceived: 'Bad company ruins good morals'" I Corinthians 15:33 (RSV).[3]

There is no way around it. It is biblical--and it is a fact of life, evidenced by many people's reason for a wandering son (or daughter): "He just got in with the wrong crowd." Nearly everybody in the world believes that, that is what happens when children are together.

I love what Jonathan Lindvall[4] says about foolish children influencing foolish children. He says that it is not that he is afraid your child will corrupt my child; it is that he is afraid that your fool will influence my fool and my fool will influence your fool. All children have the tendency to be foolish and influence others with that foolishness.

Yet parenting in fear is still the opposite of how we are to live. Furthermore, fear drives us to respond unreasonably. Fear causes us to keep our children at home and never allow them to be around anyone else. It causes us to micromanage our teens for much longer than is needed--forcing them to be unable to make decisions for themselves. It makes them miss out on opportunities that teens and young people need in their lives as they are growing into adulthood. It prevents them from developing the ability to be a friend to anyone outside of our family (and, in turn, not have the ability to influence people for the kingdom of God). We should be wary of dangers to our children, but we should parent in wisdom, not in fear.

Missing Out

Many families who overly protect their kids keep them from some outstanding opportunities that would probably have a tremendously positive influence on them, especially in the late teen years. Our answer to this, as you will read below, is to do things with your children--like conferences, ministry opportunities, and speech and debate--until you are confident in their faith and ability to be "on their own."

Many families who do not allow their students to be in speech and debate, serve in a ministry, attend a worldview conference, take a community class like desk top publishing, etc. want to protect their kids but are not willing to make the sacrifices to replace the missing activities or take part in things along with their children. The parent's thought of giving up a whole day on Saturday from repairing the house or tending to the little ones actually causes many "protected" kids to simply miss out on truly worthwhile endeavors that would help prepare them for a future of serving God and others.

False Sense of Security

Another danger of overly protecting kids, one that we have had to watch out for ourselves, is that of a false sense of security. Because our children are not with other children a lot, wear what we tell them to wear, listen to what we want them to listen to, etc., we feel secure in their future of serving God. We begin to think that these outward behaviors are indicative of inward conditions, and we fail to look deeper.

For instance, I have seen many young girls wearing just the clothes their parents want them to, having hairstyles and cosmetic applications that are acceptable in their family, playing sacred and classical music only, and many other things their parents deem as appropriate--with completely untrained hearts. I have watched these gals roll their eyes at their fathers and pull away when their mothers try to put their arm around them. They are following the external rules, those that are measurable to the outside world, yet their hearts are hard and un-pliable. And because they are following the externals--and protected from others--parents think all is well when in reality things are far from well.

Well-Socialized With Adults and Children

Overly protective parents will often cite the fact that their children are able to communicate and interact with adults and small children. They feel that their children are truly able to be social with all ages because of this. And yet, those same "socialized" young people who can interact well with adults and care for small children excellently have nothing to say to someone of their own age.

I have met children who could not carry on a conversation with another young person--some who have never heard of their state's sports teams, do not know who their governor is, and cannot discuss cultural or worldview issues with other teens--much less hair styles, music, or hobbies. Some of these parents cite this as something to be proud of--*my child is so secluded that he does not even know about the "things of the world"* (like our situation with Joshua and Santa).

Is that what it means to be "in the world but not of it"? To other young people, that unsocialized teen is not in the world at all. He is unable to reach out to others with the gospel because he cannot relate to them on any level. Other teens often steer clear of these types because they view them as "weird." We do not see this as being well-socialized at all. The ability to interact with adults and small children is noble, but not being able to interact with those of your own age is simply poor socialization.

EXTREME 2: "NORMAL" SOCIALIZATION

The other socialization trap we see is that of "normal" socialization. In our cottage classes, we have well over one hundred homeschooled students come through each year. We have seen all types of socialization models in these kids. A downward trend we are seeing in homeschooling is that of raising our children in what many parents see as a more "normal" way, resulting in teens without strong relationships with their parents and God, with excessive peer dependence, and with little character (and oftentimes a shortage in morals as well).

Peer Dependency

As stated in the first extreme, everybody knows that kids influence kids. I am amazed at the homeschooling parents who raise their children just like children who go to school, except for the fact that their kids do school at home. I know some homeschooled teens who actually spend more free time with their peers than students who go to school do because they begin hanging out at noon, as soon as their token four classes are done for the day, rather than waiting until school gets out at three o'clock.

There have been discipline situations at field trips, church, and other places in which my children have related to me that the homeschooled kids were the ones who had to be pulled out, had to leave for the day, or were asked to not come back at all. Homeschooling is supposed to be an avenue for raising children for the Lord. When the homeschooled kids are the ones causing trouble or having the negative influence, something is very wrong.

When we participate in drama, debate, and other homeschooling activities, I am saddened to see the young ladies flirting with the boys, dressing provocatively, and being catty towards other girls. I am upset to find young men being mean to the "weaker" student on the basketball court, making fun of the little kids, and talking derogatively about girls.

The Bible, research, and society all prove that when children are with peers too much in unstructured environments (especially before they are ready), peer dependency takes place. It is such a natural occurrence that most parents of children in school expect it to happen--and hope and pray their children will choose "good" kids to befriend, yet lament that there is nothing that can be done about it.

We can do something about it. And we should. There is no reason for us to stand by and watch our children become negatively affected by peers. It should not be that we expect and allow our children to become peer dependent. We have other options. We are homeschoolers who can direct our children's education, and socialization, in a way that helps them choose the right paths.

Lack of Concern for Others

Parenting our children with excessive peer influences is one of the major hindrances to the well-trained heart, as well as most other aspects of godly living and character. Others trying to capture your child's heart--steal it from you, if you will--and then pouring into it what they have in theirs is extremely dangerous. Some more progressive Christian family authors feel that this is just "fear" parenting (as described in the isolation model). However, it is not just a matter of fearing what could happen; it is a fact of what truly takes place--the very things we are told in Scripture to protect our children from.

It is rare to find a young person whose daily life revolves around peers have a genuine concern for others. Peer groups have a tendency to cause a child to look inward--into the group and into oneself--rather than outward. The world of a child saturated in peers is often extremely small and revolves around that child and his friends, as opposed to revolving around others.

THE WELL-TRAINED HEART SOCIALIZATION

We have been homeschooling for twenty-four years as of fall 2007, and through the years we have joined one bandwagon or another, one extreme or another, as most long-term homeschoolers have done. There was a time when we only ate healthfully--you know, grind your own spelt, make the bread, then make the croutons for the salad with leaf lettuce from your garden; no sugar; bean sprouts growing in the window; the whole nine yards. Then, because we were so sick of health foods, we went to the other extreme where we only ate junk--fast food, ice cream, pop, pizza. Then in time, we came back to some semblance of balance.

We went through stages in many areas--no videos to videos most evenings; no textbooks to nearly all textbooks; and on and on. In just about every area, I am happy to report, we have come back to some sort of middle ground, back to what truly worked for our family.

However, there is one thing that we have remained steadfast on, that we see as so significant, and that children's hearts are lost and won in the most--that is the idea of proper protection and socialization of our children. The remainder of this chapter will detail what we see as the well-trained heart approach to socialization and what we believe with all of our hearts to be superior to the "extreme isolationism" and the "normal socialization" models.

Socialization Must Be Taught

There are so many things in life that we take for granted that children will just catch--how to worship and love God with all their hearts, how to resolve conflicts, how to treat people, and how to interact with people, plus much more. Just because there are not formal curricula abounding for these aspects of life does not mean that they are automatically learned by children. Look around you--how many adults do you know who do not have a grasp on these basic aspects of social living?

We have set out in our parenting to purposely, individually, and biblically teach our children proper socialization. They have all needed it. Out of our four oldest children, each one has had socialization issues that he or she needed guidance in. Each one had areas of socialization that would have resulted in some aspects of ineffectiveness as Christian adults. These difficulties would not have just "gone away" or improved without our help. Joshua went through a period of time in junior high in which he was consumed with two things: sports and politics (government). When he was with people, he would inappropriately, consistently steer the conversation to one of "his" areas. Obviously, this was a form of selfishness coming through, but he honestly did not set out to make everybody talk about what he was into. It just always seemed to happen. It took a conscientious effort on his part, along with our instruction in the negativity of this social interaction, to correct it.

Kayla went through a "look what I know" stage when she was eleven or twelve. Everything that was said reminded her of something she knew. If we were playing cards at a family gathering, we would find Kayla explaining all about the queens of England who found themselves either beheaded or dumped by King Henry VIII. If water was boiling on the stove, we would overhear her explaining the properties of liquids, solids, and vapors to her grandparents. It was annoying and unwelcome by most people. To her, there was nothing wrong with it. After all, these people didn't know about English history or chemistry; she could help educate them. We found relatives rolling their eyes and other kids sighing and changing the subject (or avoiding her altogether). This was socially unacceptable behavior that needed removed from Kayla's life. How would she have known if we had not gently and tenderly (most of the time!) taught her that it was not desired socialization? How could she have changed if we did not help her see when it was happening and help her discern other people's responses to her?

Cami went through a stage when she was around ten or eleven in which she did and said things in order to get attention. She talked loudly, laughed inappropriately, and tried to steer conversations and attention to herself. How could she have corrected this antisocial behavior if we had not told her that if she wants attention or needs someone to talk to, she should come to us and we would give it to her? How could she have acted more socially correct if we had not caught her in the middle of these behaviors and whispered in her ear, "Cami, you don't need to be like this to get people to notice you. We love you just the way you are. If you need attention, come to Mommy--don't act like that in front of others to get attention"?

Kara realized the plight of the middle child and felt all alone after her older brother married and her two older sisters, whom she had spent nearly all of her time with, went to college and ministries every day all of a sudden. She went through a lengthy socialization issue of "nobody likes me; I'm untalented; Joshua, Kayla, and Cami have all of the intelligence and talents." She was timid with people and felt embarrassed to talk to others because of her feelings of inferiority. What would have happened if we had not made it of primary importance to talk to Kara about this constantly and encourage her that she did have much to offer in the areas of skills and personality? How well would she have been socialized if we had not made a concentrated effort to help her find her niche in ministry and service for others?

Talking only about your interests, showing off knowledge, acting out to get attention, and the inability to talk to others (due to inferiority issues) are all significant socialization weaknesses. Proper socialization is not just gained through osmosis. It must be taught, trained, corrected, and instilled. It is of utmost importance for our children's future impact on the world that they not continue into adulthood with socialization issues that could have been resolved if we had taken the time and effort to help them correct them. It is vital to the kingdom of God--and we consider it part of our job description as parents.

Replace Peers With Something Better

When Cami was eighteen, she pulled me and Ray off to the side as we were leaving one evening to go speak to a homeschooling group. The conversation went something like this:

> Cami: Are you guys going to talk about socialization tonight?
>
> Me: Probably; we usually end up there somehow.

Cami: Well, when you do, do you think you could, like, um, well...not make it seem like we live in a box so much? I mean, tell them we're cool, and we have cool clothes, cool hair, and cool jewelry, and things, okay?

Me: Cami, before you began ministry school as a high school senior, at age seventeen, how many evenings a month did you do things with others that did not involve your siblings and/or parents?

Cami: Hmm...well, I don't know. Not many that I can think of.

Me: Exactly.

Cami: Ahhh...help....I did live in a box!

We fully believe what the Bible (and *The Socialization Trap*) teaches about fools influencing fools and bad companions corrupting others. However, like other things we removed from our children's lives, we believe that if you remove excessive peer influence from your child's life (as we did to a large extent in the early years), you need to replace it with something. We replaced it with ourselves.

We followed a healthy protection approach with our children up to their late teen years. By healthy protection, I mean that we protected our children from too much peer interaction by limiting their friendships to family friends and limiting their interactions to those involving meaningful activities and hospitality times. They were taught from early ages that their brothers and sisters are their best friends--and that if they can get along with their siblings, they will be set for outstanding relationships their entire lives.

However, unlike the "extreme isolation model" of socialization, we did not just keep them away from others. We limited their peer interaction, substituted ourselves for peers, and allowed interaction with others with us there. From get-togethers at our house after a speech tournament to several years of debate classes, club, and tournaments--we did not keep them away from everyone; we allowed them to be with people all the time, to learn excellent communication skills, and to have frames of reference for lively family discussions later. We provided what we believe were safe and proper socialization opportunities--and taught them how to interact with others as we went along.

Proper Socialization Is Developed With Healthy Protection Followed by Gradual Release

Our children are so socially adjusted that people are often surprised to learn that our younger children (under sixteen or seventeen, depending on gender and maturity) do not spend a lot of time at friends' houses, stay overnight with others, do things separate from each other, etc., but instead spend time with their parents or siblings nearly every weekend. It is because we did not just pull them out of society in an effort to protect them. We held them back from negative situations (fools influencing fools) then gradually released them as they showed maturity enough to handle various situations.

When we *have* released our children to be around peers more, it was not to go "hang out." It was because they were ready to be launched into aggressive part time ministry. They were ready to go out and serve in the "uttermost parts of the world"--having proven themselves faithful at home and in service and ministry with us. We protected them from negative influences during the years that they were "children"--the years they thought as children, the years they were foolish, the years their peers were foolish--until they no longer thought as children. At that time, our children are ready to "go ye into all the world" without fear of influences since we used their homeschooling years wisely. They are trained. They are ready. They are socialized.

Protect Without Offending

I need to end this socialization chapter with a major caution: do not offend others as you seek to protect your children. Too many people alienate their church friends, offend their neighbors, and hurt their relatives in an effort to protect their children. Obviously, if it came to a decision as to have your children in harm's way or offend someone, there is no question. But most homeschoolers who try to protect their children from peers need to learn more graciousness in doing so.

We lived in a neighborhood for a few years when our seven children were between the ages of newborn through fourteen. We had worked too hard to just suddenly let peers (neighbor kids) come in and influence our children, but at the same time, we did not want to offend our neighbors and come across "holier than thou."

So we made a policy that the neighbor kids were welcome at our house anytime Ray and I were outside with the children. They were not to come over until we were out playing or working with the kids. Then they were more than welcome to come over and join in our family activities--kickball, four square, basketball, etc. This worked well as they loved to play family games with us, and we were not shutting them out entirely.

One Sunday afternoon when Ray and I were taking a nap, I heard a knock on the front door.

The next thing I heard was one of the neighbor boys talking to Joshua:

> "Can your dad come out to play?"
>
> Joshua: No, he's taking a nap, but when he gets up, I'll tell him that you want him to come play.
>
> An hour later, I heard another knock, same kid---"Is your dad up yet? Could you go wake him up and see if he wants to play?"

We can protect our children, teach them proper socialization, and be a light to our neighbors all at the same time. It takes more from us, of course, but everything that is good takes more.

We can also avoid *both* socialization traps. It will again take more work and effort than we ever dreamed. It will require yielding still more of our time and desires. It will mean planning and prioritizing yet another aspect of our family's life in order to succeed. However, we can provide proper, healthy socialization that results in children who are ready to be "witnesses to the world for a lifetime" because we have "protected them from the world for a short time."

"The Socialization Trap**s**"
Discussion/Application Questions
--- Chapter 13 ---

1. Do you feel that you must adopt the school's socialization approach in order to have truly socialized children? Why do you think this? What positive socialization do you see from that approach?
2. What is your definition of proper socialization? What do you want your kids' socialization to look like when they are grown?
3. In what ways do you parent in fear? How do they affect your approach to homeschooling and socialization?
4. Do your children miss out on important things that God may desire for them because of your isolation? If so, how can you give these opportunities to your kids while still protecting them the way you feel you should?
5. Are your children well socialized with all ages of people?
6. What is your view of peer dependency? Do you think it is a danger to your family? If so, in what ways?
7. How are you purposefully teaching socialization to your children? What social deficiencies do you see in them? How can you counter-act these?
8. How do you feel about healthy protection followed by gradual release of older teens? Do you think this approach could help you meet your homeschooling and socialization goals?

FOURTEEN

What a Smarty Pants!

Academics and the Well-Trained Heart

Throughout *The Well-Trained Heart*, we have focused primarily on just that--how to train the heart well. However, a book about "homeschooling" must have a chapter on academics, so here it is!

I have purposely not included too much information about our kids' academic achievements. Oh, they have them. Many of them, in fact. However, we did not want to detract from the WTH message by focusing on scholarly successes early in the book.

Joshua graduated from high school with a near 4.0 grade point average and then went on to test out of nearly all of his college degree in history. (He only took two classes, classes that did not have any CLEP tests available.) And yes, he graduated from college with honors too.

Kayla also had a near 4.0 GPA in high school, then proceeded to get a perfect score on the verbal portions of the ACT, not once, but twice! She is an honors student at Indiana-Purdue University in Fort Wayne (IPFW), Indiana in nursing and an honors student at a Bible college as well. Oh, she attends IPFW on a full ride academic scholarship.

Cami began college during her junior year of high school and now works half time as the disability ministry director at our church while she attends Bible college (where she has an outstanding GPA as well). She actually takes classes from two Bible colleges, one for her major (general church ministry) and one for her minor (disability ministry).

All three of them have advanced to the national speech and debate tournament in the NCFCA[1] numerous times in many events, and both of the girls placed at the national level in various speech categories. (Joshua got started too late in high school, so our club did not have the speech portion of the NCFCA league at that time.)

Our younger children are following suit. Kara is going for a 4.0 on her high school transcript and will attend college as a high school senior. Jonathan will only have one high school class remaining at the end of his ninth grade year. All of the five oldest children, so far, have had twice as many high school credits as is mandatory in our state, mostly due to their independent studies in their areas of interest (sign language, Spanish, writing, history, literature, editing, desk top publishing, piano, home economics, etc.).

Those are some of our children's academic achievements--even though some of them would be considered "average" intellectually, and one of them is severely dyslexic and dysgraphic.
How did they end up with such scholarly achievements if they are not all "geniuses"? How did they end up with such high academic successes while we emphasized heart training? It is *because* we

emphasized heart training that they have achieved so much scholastically. Again, we believe there are certain orders in life, and if we "seek first the kingdom of God,"[2] the other needed things will be added.

HOMESCHOOL BEGINNINGS

The Well-Trained Heart Approach Affects All Areas

Notice I said *needed* things are added. We have found that when we have lived the well-trained heart approach and put relationship with God and others and character above academics, we were able to easily add in what each child needed for his or her future.

You see, life is not made up of separate "compartments." Everything is interrelated. That is equally true with homeschooling. The parenting and child training approach you adopt carries over into your school. The importance you place on heart training influences how, why, when, and where you homeschool.

When we say we are living the well-trained heart approach to homeschooling, we are saying that God is first, relationships with others and character training are next. Academics are important, yes, but only as a vehicle to being successful in serving God.

In living this lifestyle, our belief that each of our children needs a good foundational education (math, writing, social studies, science, health, etc.) is the basis for our school curriculum. Then, as we live closely in relationship with our children, we see bents, strengths, weaknesses, callings, interests, and lacks of interest. All of these help us determine where each child will head educationally as he enters junior high, high school, and even college.

Whose Job Is It?

A couple of years ago Ray and I were especially disturbed to see so many moms being solely responsible for the education of their children via homeschooling. I commented that if I heard another man say, "Yes, my wife homeschools," I was going to throw something at him. (Okay, that wasn't the best example before my children nor was it good character training!)

Well, our three young sons were especially in tune with this dilemma and reported to us often about dads who were taking active roles in their homeschools and dads who were not. Once when we were speaking and vending at a homeschooling convention, our sons enjoyed "window shopping" at all of the booths. They hurriedly came back to us, out of breath, exclaiming, "We found the problem, Mom. There is a booth here with a man actually passing out stickers that say, 'My wife homeschools, and she's my hero'!"

They were sure that they had found the culprit to this dad problem--Todd Wilson, of FamilyMan Ministries,[3] was encouraging dads to make their wives do all of the work--and distributing stickers to promote it! Of course, that is not what FamilyMan Ministries is about, and Todd Wilson is doing a great work for dads and homeschooling. However, it was a comical look at this problem of "wives homeschooling."

We have laid the foundation for the well-trained heart in this book with the responsibility on both Mom and Dad to train their children's hearts well. We believe the same is true of academics. At the very least, moms and dads need to work together to develop their children's academic program.

Actually, there is a New Testament verse that points to the fact that dads, not moms, are ultimately responsible for the scholastic training of their children. Galatians 4: 2 indicates that New Testament dads determined when and how a child would be educated: "But is under tutors and governors until the time appointed of the father (KJV)."[4]

We are not big fans of the "this is the husband's job" and "this is the wife's job" approach for things that are not clearly laid out in Scripture. We usually work within our strengths and time constraints for "undesignated" jobs. However, we definitely believe that the education of our children is both parents' responsibility, not just the mother's.

How this takes place in each individual home will be different. Many things come into play for this, including the academic strengths of both parents, the ages of the children, the load that each parent carries (the wife with the house and number of children and possibly part time work and the husband with his job), the extent of each child's education, and much more.

For example, when our older children were younger, my full time job was homemaking and homeschooling. I did the majority of "academics" with the children. I also made most of the decisions concerning curriculum and scheduling. Ray and I would talk it over, but ultimately, I was the one teaching, so he trusted my judgment. During this time, he worked a lot, so I did not ask him to grade papers, do math drills, or teach reading. However, he did extensive Bible and character training with the children in the mornings and the evenings. We tried to utilize him to do the most important things with the limited time that he had.

Now that we have started our homeschooling ministry and publishing company,[5] we both work many hours building up the business and making money to live on (and making money to support the business until it can stand on its own). The teaching of our children is spread out among Ray, our older children, outside teachers, and me. Ray, our older kids, and I all teach cottage classes (enrichment classes for homeschoolers) that our children participate in. Thus, in the past four years, Ray has taught speech, debate, economics, and accounting through these classes. He has also taught driver's education and math to our children. Additionally, he has helped me with Jacob's reading and speech therapy, as well as extensive discipleship of our older children. And he continues to teach Bible, character, discipleship, and other "read aloud" things with the younger children a few times a week.

Our young adults also teach cottage classes that our younger ones take. Thus, our middle school and high school students get instruction in many of their classes from their older siblings, including literature, history, government, apologetics, biology, chemistry, speech, debate, and Spanish. Also, Kara, Jonathan, and Josiah have assignments each day to work with Jacob on various areas (phonics, reading aloud, Bible reading, etc.). We have hired teachers in piano, voice, guitar, sewing, and Spanish (prior to Kayla's teaching of it).

Additionally, we use independent study for many subjects. We have trained our children to study, learn, research, manage time, etc. so that they can learn on their own, as well. Most of their math, math drill, and history are independent study.

What does all of this have to do with the well-trained heart approach to homeschooling? Our children's education should not all fall on Mom's shoulders. At the very least, Dad should be an integral part of the decision making, Bible, and discipleship. He should never tell people that "his wife homeschools" unless, of course, it is to tell people that "she is his hero"!

Better Late Than Early

I mentioned earlier that we first learned of homeschooling through Dr. Raymond Moore's writings. Two of his books that influenced me early in our homeschooling are entitled *Better Late Than Early*[6] and *School Can Wait.*[7] The thing that initially struck me the most about Dr. Moore's books is how consistent they were with research. I had just graduated with a teaching degree the week before I read his books. I was amazed how so much of what he had written was what I had learned in college!

The biggest difference between what I had learned in college and Dr. Moore's teaching is that we were told in college that yes, these things are true: boys mature later academically than girls, many children are not ready to learn to read at age six or seven, etc; but there is nothing you can do about in school. My classmates and I were told to "just do the best you can in your classroom while keeping the research in mind." Dr. Moore's books said the same things about how children learn, but told us we could do something about it; we could homeschool.

We are not unschooling proponents, and we don't even think that all children need to "wait" to start school. However, we have found Dr. Moore's advice to wait until children are ready to learn to read and write before attempting to teach them more "academic" subjects to be extremely consistent with the well-trained heart approach.

With the WTH approach, we look at each individual child in determining his homeschooling program. It does not involve a "one size fits all" approach. Boys are often behind girls academically. Because I know this, and because I want my boys to enjoy learning and school, I do not push them to learn to read at age six or seven (unless they show definite readiness to learn at that age).

Boys catch up with girls eventually, and everything shakes out in the end, but in protecting their hearts from unnecessary failure and stresses, we wait until our children (boys *and* girls) are ready for more academic learning before beginning it.

Our Story: Kayla's Dyslexia

I can hardly bear to think about where at least two of our children would be academically and emotionally if they had gone to school--and even if we had homeschooled them without considering their readiness and weaknesses. The well-trained heart approach has made a huge difference in the life of our extremely gifted dyslexic Kayla. I want to share her story here because it illuminates so many of the positive effects of the WTH approach on academic learning.

First of all, you must understand that at the time Kayla became school age, I was nearly finished with a reading specialist's master's degree. I was two classes away from this degree, yet I had no idea how to help my daughter learn to read. This is important to note because many homeschooling moms who are not "trained teachers" tend to think that if they had gone to college for teaching, they would know how to teach. In college (and even in graduate school), I learned how to use textbooks, how to manage a classroom, and how to group students. I did not learn how to teach one-on-one. I learned that through teaching my own kids and tutoring other students.

When Kayla was little, she was a late talker and had speech difficulties when she did learn to talk. As she neared school age, I had already adopted the "better late than early" mindset in terms of not pressuring little children to learn before they are ready, and waiting on academics in an effort to build a love for learning and school in my young students. So, when Kayla was not ready to learn to read at ages six and seven, I was not surprised or even concerned. She was extremely intelligent, could remember everything, comprehended what she heard way beyond her years, and loved learning.

As she neared age eight, and I was attempting to teach her to read with what was considered the "cadillac" of reading programs, things were still not clicking for her. I again waited a few more months, and by the time she was ten, she was reading chapter books.

Even though she had severe reversal problems (and now I know many other symptoms of dyslexia), I didn't think much of her as a "dyslexic" because I still believed, incorrectly, that dyslexics were not very smart. I didn't see how she could be dyslexic since she was so intelligent, and since she did, eventually, learn to read fluently.

However, from ages nine to thirteen, her dyslexia (and dysgraphia, difficulties with writing/penning) became obvious and caused her a lot of problems with writing and spelling. Even though she could read at a high school level and comprehend at a post high school level, she could not spell simple words, such as *when* and *how*, and she could not write legibly, despite multiple and intensive handwriting lessons and books.

Now, mind you, we did have our moments (like making her sit at the table all evening until she wrote a paragraph one time when she was twelve), but for the most part, because we believed that unnecessary pressure and the "one size fits all" educational program would hurt Kayla, we adjusted our school to compensate for her difficulties. We did phonics, spelling, and penmanship extensively until she was fourteen. At that time, she continued to do spelling and penmanship on her own until her high school graduation as she sincerely desired to overcome these difficulties. (It was actually quite comical during her senior year of high school when she would go to college in the mornings, then come home and do a primary penmanship book in the afternoons.)

Kayla was extremely intelligent and creative, so I spent huge amounts of time allowing her to dictate her reports, stories, and essays to me as I typed them on the computer or penned them in her notebook. Before she was reading fluently, we used other avenues of learning (besides the traditional "read the textbook and answer the questions"). We used large amounts of audio materials, teaching tapes, books on tape, radio dramas, etc. We also used some video teaching. Oh, and I read to her--for hours every day.

Kayla still suffers the effects of dyslexia on her spelling and dysgraphia on her writing. Thankfully, when she was thirteen, we taught her to type extensively and use spell-check, and by the time she was fifteen, she was writing elementary language arts curriculum. (She would ask her little brothers how to spell the words she was putting into the second and third grade curriculum!) Once she could type, her world changed immensely. The two biggest obstacles to her academic success were gone or greatly lessened, that of not being able to spell and not being able to write legibly.

Things were not smooth easy sailing from the time Kayla learned to type, of course. She had difficulties learning to drive due to her perception of how close vehicles were to her and her inability to tell her left from her right. (After hitting three parked cars within the first few months of driving, she decided that driving a full-sized van was out of the question for her!) She had to train for months to prepare for the SAT and ACT exams, in large part because words and numbers in isolation (i.e. those not in a sentence, but those in vocabulary lists and numerals in math problems) are difficult for her to decipher and cause her to miss questions unnecessarily. She has also had difficulty in all types of formal testing due to the "color in the space" approach; she loses her place on them easily. More recently, she has had extreme frustration learning to spell all of the drugs in her pharmacology classes. She has to put in two or three times the amount of time and effort in studying these as even her less intelligent peers do.

You can see from this story why I mourned for days when Dr. Raymond Moore passed away last year. His work literally changed Kayla's life. If she had been in school, she would have been in special education and lost in the system, probably still unable to write today. If we had not adopted Dr. Moore's teaching, she could hate learning and school today (instead of adoring it more than any other young person I know). We could have developed strained relationships with her as we pushed and pushed for her to "just get it." And she would not be preparing today to "go ye into all the world."

From our experience with Kayla, we learned the importance of waiting on readiness, developing each child's school program with that child's strengths and weaknesses in mind, and doing whatever it takes to insure success (reading aloud and typing for her for several years). This is the well-trained heart approach to education. The focus is on the whole child and on the relationship of that child with her parents and with God.

THE WELL-TRAINED HEART AND SCHOOL CHILDREN

Faith, Virtue, Knowledge

In "How We Found the Well-Trained Heart," we mentioned that we were influenced by the verse in II Peter: "But also for this very reason, giving all diligence, add to your faith virtue, to virtue knowledge" II Peter 1:5 (NKJV).[8] This became the basis for creating our school schedule each day, deciding what classes we would study and how much time we would spend on them, and even when our children started formal academics.

First of all, this verse became the order for our days. If faith is the most important thing to us, we should begin our school day with the Bible and biblical teaching. Thus, throughout the years, we have had devotions together, and the children have done individual devotions, at the beginning of the day. If virtue (or character) is the next most important thing, we should focus on that following faith. In a practical sense, this means completing chores and household responsibilities. For us, it has also meant studying character qualities and godly people. Thus, we have a morning reading time in which we learn about character through character stories and discipleship types of books. We also study godly people to see how they have lived out the Christian life. We do this by reading biographies each day. Then we are ready to begin academic subjects.

As to this verse's influence on what we study and how much time we spend on subjects, we have had to make decisions to cut out other subjects in an effort to keep faith and virtue in the schedule. We have had to switch programs, for example, when we realized a child's math was taking more time each day than what we spent on faith and virtue. Math should not take two hours a day for elementary children!

Lastly, we have never felt that a child should "do school" when he was still severely lacking in character. What makes us think a young student will sit and do language arts lessons when he will not brush his teeth? Why would a child do math drills when he will not come when he is called? Again, we have found there is a hierarchy in skills. To push academics when a child is still disobedient, irresponsible, or lazy seems useless to us. During that time, he needs a focus on obedience and diligence, with Mom providing close supervision and follow through.

Accountability for School and Chores

Children need accountability in order to gain the character qualities of responsibility, resourcefulness, diligence, and much more. Because of this, we have used printed schedules, chore charts, school checklists, etc. for our children. The goal of all parenting is to raise our children to be independent in all areas of their lives (actually, independent of us, but dependent upon the Lord). This never happens when we are spoon-feeding their school to them, giving them "token" chores, and generally making everything easy on them as they grow up. Just like children need a gradual release from us socially, emotionally, and spiritually, they also need a gradual release academically.

One thing that we would never do without in our homeschool is the "morning routine." I always tell moms that if they would implement this one aspect of scheduling into their homeschools, they would notice an immediate difference in many areas, including independence and diligence. The morning routine is a checklist that our children have to do each morning before anything else. (This has been before and after our morning devotions and readings, depending on Mom and Dad's schedules.) Based on the ages of our children, this has included cleaning their bedrooms, making their beds, showering/grooming, putting away pj's and

books from the night before, and doing devotions.
Following the morning routine charts, we use a chore schedule that has each child responsible for various chores at his level three times a day. For example, a seven year old might unload the dishes, reload the dishes, and set the table before breakfast. He might empty all trash cans and help fix lunch before lunch. Before dinner, he might unload the dishes, reload the dishes, sweep the porch, and set the table. Three chore times a day with everyone working in his areas insures that all daily work gets done.

Then we have used school checklists for each child's independent work. When the children were unable to read, we made picture charts showing anything they were to do for school on their own each day, such as Geosafari,[9] computer math drills, book and tape sets, etc. While this is not a "heavy" academic load, it does start making our children responsible for some aspects of their school each day early on.

As the kids have advanced in their school grades, their school checklist becomes more and more detailed. Everything they need to do each day, plus any "homework" they have assigned from our "tutoring sessions" together goes on it. These checklists have helped our children learn responsibility. They have also helped the children learn how to learn on their own. Of course, from conflicts and difficulties with following through on their checklists and "lessons" from us, they have learned time management principles and prioritizing.

Learning Together

We believe that homeschoolers should homeschool in the way that best suits their family's situation (number of students, number of little kids, availability of Mom, Dad's work schedule, etc.). We also believe that each child's education should be tailored to him, especially as children get into junior high and high school. However, we have also found that learning together is conducive to the furtherance of heart training in our children.

The extent to the "learning together" approach for each family will be different, too. For us, we continue to do a lot of Bible, character, and discipleship type of learning together up through high school. As mentioned earlier, we even do studies and discipleship with our college students.

We have enjoyed unit studies with our elementary and junior high children from the beginning. We love to read history, creation science, literature, and biographies together. As our students get older, they get their own history and science books, and they join us less and less. For example, I do creation science books and story time with our twelve and nine year olds, but our ninth and eleventh graders do their own science (chemistry with Kayla).

I am saddened to see moms who feel inferior in their homeschools say things like, "I am just not the 'unit study' type of mom." Unit studies have become a sort of idol for many homeschoolers, and this should not be. Unit studies are a means (an approach) to an end (a good education). If your children each have their own science and history books, but you enjoy Bible and biographies together, you are still utilizing the strong oral approach as well as tying heart strings. It does not have to be an "all or nothing" proposal in order to enjoy the benefits of learning together.

Delight Directed Studies

Another homeschooling concept that we adopted from Gregg Harris[10] is that of delight directed studies. In this approach, we look for our children's special interests and bents, and teach him, or allow him to learn independently about that interest. When Joshua was in elementary school and junior high, he was crazy about sports cards and sports teams. He would organize his cards into teams, based on each player's positions, statistics, etc. Ray picked up on this and would often do math with him with his sports cards. (To this day, Joshua says he only passed the statistics CLEP test because his dad taught him about statistics and probability with sports cards on the living room floor and free throws in the driveway!)

We have done this extensively with our children. The girls wanted to sew and quilt, and we used those opportunities to teach geometry. Cami desired to learn sign language, so we got her into a sign language class, and she attended deaf church in high school to further this. The boys practically create their own "unit studies" now with their extensive coin collecting. They continually look up dates, people, and places online, study maps of certain time periods, and more to expand their coin collecting endeavor.

We have found that paying attention to our children's interests and bents as they approach high school is especially important. Sure, in elementary and junior high, they may enjoy many things, but if those interests persist into high school, they could very well have something to do with their futures. This has been true in Cami's life with sign language and working with the deaf, and it has been true for Kayla with her Spanish development. Joshua's years and years of map making with highlighters and poster boards were simply the beginning of his love for and eventually, his college degree in history. All of our children's interests in speech have aided their future. Cami and Kayla speak and teach at church constantly. Joshua, Kayla, and Cami all speak with us at conventions and conferences.

THE WELL-TRAINED HEART AND OLDER STUDENTS

Helping Older Students Become Responsible for Their Learning

Sir Walter Scott once said, "All men who have turned out worth anything have had the chief hand in their own education." We have the potential to teach our children how to learn, to make them responsible for part of their education, and to help them become life-long learners. As Scott alluded to, when our children (especially our teens) have a major role in their schooling, it becomes more important to them; it has more of an impact on their future success.

Some of the tips in the elementary section have had a large bearing on our children becoming responsible for their school--giving them independent work to be done each day, utilizing school checklists, providing some curricula and school materials that are self-study (as opposed to needing Mom in all subjects), providing accountability for their work. However, as our children have gotten into junior high and high school, we have found an even greater need to put some of the responsibility for their school onto them. We have done this a number of ways. The school checklists continue in junior high and high school, but I like to sit down with the students and have them help determine what their days will look like, what they need to do each day, etc. Of course, this is strong training in study skills--mapping out how long it takes to complete a certain amount of work, fitting it into the schedule, etc.

Along the same lines, we like to sit down with our children in junior high and high school and decide what they will study for the year, what their goals are for that year. Obviously, some subjects are automatic, based on your state's mandates and your family's schooling styles. However, once we get beyond the *you need another year of English comp; you need to complete Algebra II, and you need another year of world history*, then we can talk about goals, strengths, and interests. This has resulted in the aforementioned Spanish, sign language, piano, voice, quilting, sewing, and advanced math classes (for Kayla). Jonathan is eagerly awaiting the day he is done with his biology and Chemistry (requirements that he will complete his freshman year) so that he can study astronomy and marine biology. Again, the more input they have into their school and their goals, the more likely they are to enjoy school and learning and meet their goals.

The idea of completing their checklist each day for junior high and high school students points directly back to the child discipline areas. If our children do not obey us in smaller things of life, they are not likely to complete a daily school list in junior high or high school. If you have not made your children responsible for daily school lists (and chore lists), you will have to be firm and consistent with them. School and work are to be done before play. Just like the two-year-old who knows you will not really make him sit at the table through the whole meal if he yells loudly enough and throws his drink frequently enough, the older student knows whether he will really get to do what he wants each afternoon or evening if he doesn't get his list done. If you have not made him responsible for things earlier, it will be difficult as he gets older, but it is a huge stepping stone to success in life and in living for the Lord, and is worth the hassle, time, and effort to make it happen.

School Is Student's "Occupation"

We mentioned this earlier, but because of the laxness we have seen in the past several years of tutoring, it bears repeating. Learning is what children are supposed to do! Our high schooler's education, whether it is academic-oriented or trades oriented, is his occupation during this time.

Making older children responsible for their school, developing a course of study that helps each child reach his potential, and developing a good, consistent schedule all contribute to this "occupation" mentality. Letting children leave things undone to go play, focus too much on jobs rather than finishing their school, and developing a lax schedule with too little learning taking place all point to a lacking in this "occupation" mentality.

So what is the key to combining heart training with strong academic learning? We believe that this key points back to prioritizing. Yes, academics are important--in that they help our children become what God wants for them to become. But academic learning is not an end in itself. The final goal of our homeschooling is not just educated children. Many forms of school produce educated students. The end goal of our homeschooling has to be that our child has the education and tools to fulfill the callings that God has on his life--and that he has a heart to love God fully and serve others selflessly.

"What a Smarty Pants!"
Discussion/Application Questions
-- Chapter 14 --

1. Do you focus more on heart training than academics?
2. Do you focus too little on academics or not fulfill your scholastic obligations (according to your state)?
3. As a husband, do you view homeschooling as your wife's job? How can you begin to take the responsibility for your children's education? How can you relieve your wife's pressure in your homeschool?
4. Have you put too much pressure on your children for areas that are out of their control (i.e. readiness to learn to read, ability to spell well, etc.)?
5. How can you begin to tailor your homeschool to each individual child's bents and interests?
6. What order do you place faith, virtue, and knowledge in during your homeschool day? What effect do these things have on your school schedule and curriculum choices?
7. What remedial character training do you need to do with your younger children to prepare them to "do school"?
8. How could morning routines help you have more successful school days?
9. What types of accountability systems can you implement to help your children start being responsible for their school work?
10. How can you start learning together?
11. What areas of interest do you see in your children that could become delight-directed studies?

End Notes

Chapter 1: Don't Go Breakin' My Heart

1. Home page. *Barna Research Group*. Online. Accessed 31 October 2007: www.barna.org.
2. Bradley, Reb. *Solving the Crisis in Homeschooling.* 22 September 2006: www.familyministries.com/HS_Crisis.htm.
3. "But you are a chosen generation, a royal priesthood, a holy nation, His own special people, that you may proclaim the praises of Him who called you out of darkness into His marvelous light;" 1 Peter 2:9 (NKJV).
4. "I do not understand my own actions. For I do not do what I want, but I do the very thing I hate" Romans 7:15 (RSV).
5. "He who spares his rod hates his son, but he who loves him disciplines him promptly" Proverbs 13:24 (NKJV).
6. Kimmel, Tim. *Grace-Based Parenting.* Nashville: Thomas Nelson, 2004.
7. "Now hope does not disappoint, because the love of God has been poured out in our hearts by the Holy Spirit who was given to us" Romans 5:5 (NKJV).
8. "Train up a child in the way he should go; and when he is old he will not depart from it" Proverbs 22:6 (KJV).
9. "Story of the Prodigal Son," Luke 15:13-31 (NKJV).
10. "Story of Adam and Eve," Genesis 2:4-3:24 (NKJV).

Chapter 2: Journey to the Center of the Heart

1. Home page. *Terry and Esa Everroad.* Online. Accessed 8 January 2008: www.everroad.com.
2. Home page. *Hewitt Homeschooling Resources.* Online. Accessed 31 October 2007: www.hewitthomeschooling.com.
3. Home page. *Dr. Raymond Moore.* Online. Accessed 8 January 2008: www.moorefoundation.com.
4. Coriell, Ron and Rebekah Coriell. *Child's Book of Character Building.* Grand Rapids: Revell Publishing, 1995.
5. Harris, Gregg. *The Christian Home School.* Vancouver: Noble Publishing Associates, 1988.
6. Home page. *Institute in Basic Life Principles.* Online.

Accessed 31 October 2007: http://iblp.org/iblp/.
7. Home page. *KONOS.* Online. Accessed 31 October 2007. www.konos.com.
8. "You shall love the Lord your God with all your heart, with all your soul, and with all your strength. And these words which I command you today shall be in your heart. You shall teach them diligently to your children, and shall talk of them when you sit in your house, when you walk by the way, when you lie down, and when you rise up. You shall bind them as a sign on your hand, and they shall be as frontlets between your eyes" Deuteronomy 6:5-8 (NKJV).
9. "But also for this very reason, giving all diligence, add to your faith virtue, to virtue knowledge" II Peter 1:5 (NKJV).

Chapter 3: All I Really Need to Know I Learned From Debate
1. Fulghum, Robert. *All I Really Need to Know I Learned in Kindergarten.* Raleigh: Ivy Books, 1989.
2. "Therefore, though I might be very bold in Christ to command you what is fitting, yet for love's sake I rather appeal to you---being such a one as Paul, the aged, and now also a prisoner of Jesus Christ" Philemon 1:8-9 (NKJV).
3. Home page. *National Christian Forensics and Communications Association.* Online. Accessed 31 October 2007: www.ncfca.org.
4. Shipe, Christy. *Introduction to Argumentation and Debate.* Purcellville: Home School Legal Defense, 1998.
5. Home page. *Home School Legal Defense.* Online. Accessed 31 October 2007: www.hslda.org.
6. "But in your hearts set apart Christ as Lord. Always be prepared to give an answer to everyone who asks you to give the reason for the hope that you have. But do this with gentleness and respect" I Peter 3:15 (NIV).
7. "Story of Abraham and Isaac," Genesis 22 (NKJV).

Chapter 4: Bible Heart Beat
1. "The heart is deceitful above all things, And desperately wicked; Who can know it?" Jeremiah 17:9 (NKJV).

2. "Take heed to yourselves, lest your heart be deceived, and you turn aside and serve other gods and worship them" Deuteronomy 11:16 (NKJV).
3. "You brood of snakes! How could evil men like you speak what is good and right? For whatever is in your heart determines what you say" Matthew 12:34 (NLT).
4. "And he did evil, because he did not prepare his heart to seek the Lord" II Chronicles 12:14 (NKJV).
5. Home page. *The Barna Group.* Online. Accessed 8 January 2008: www.barna.org.
6. "And he will turn The hearts of the fathers to the children. And the hearts of the children to their fathers. Lest I come and strike the earth with a curse" Malachi 4:6 (NKJV).
7. "But I have stilled and quieted my soul; like a weaned child with its mother, like a weaned child is my soul within me" Psalms 131:2 (NIV).
8. "Love never fails. But where there are prophecies, they will cease; where there are tongues, they will be stilled; where there is knowledge, it will pass away. For we know in part and we prophesy in part, but when perfection comes, the imperfect disappears. When I was a child, I talked like a child, I thought like a child, I reasoned like a child. When I became a man, I put childish ways behind me. Now we see but a poor reflection as in a mirror; then we shall see face to face. Now I know in part; then I shall know fully, even as I am fully known. And now these three remain: faith, hope and love. But the greatest of these is love" I Corinthians 13:8-13 (NIV).
9. "My son, give me your heart, And let your eyes observe my ways" Proverbs 23:26 (NKJV).
10. "Foolishness is bound up in the heart of a child; The rod of correction will drive it far from him" Proverbs 22:15 (NKJV).

Chapter 5: Let It Begin With Me

1. "He gives the barren woman a home, making her the joyous mother of children. Praise the LORD!" Psalms 113:9 (RSV).
2. "Fathers, do not exasperate your children; instead, bring

them up in the training and instruction of the Lord" Ephesians 6:4 (NIV).
3. "He will turn the hearts of the fathers to their children, and the hearts of the children to their fathers; or else I will come and strike the land with a curse" Malachi 4:6 (NIV).
4. "Do not be deceived: 'Bad company ruins good morals'" I Corinthians 15:33 (RSV).
5. "A disciple is not above his teacher, but everyone who is perfectly trained will be like his teacher" Luke 6:40 (NKJV).
6. "If anyone does not provide for his relatives, and especially for his immediate family, he has denied the faith and is worse than an unbeliever" I Timothy 5:8 (NIV).
7. "He must manage his own family well and see that his children obey him with proper respect" I Timothy 3:4 (NIV).
8. "Wives, submit to your own husbands, as to the Lord" Ephesians 5:22 (NKJV).
9. "Submitting to one another in the fear of God" Ephesians 5:21 (NKJV).
10. I Corinthians 13 (NIV).
11. "Be kind and compassionate to one another, forgiving each other, just as in Christ God forgave you" Ephesians 4:32 (NIV).
12. "But Jesus knew their thoughts, and said to them: 'Every kingdom divided against itself is brought to desolation, and every city or house divided against itself will not stand'" Matthew 12:25 (NKJV).
13. "So they are no longer two, but one. Therefore what God has joined together, let man not separate" (Matthew 19:6 NIV).
14. "No one can serve two masters; for either he will hate the one and love the other, or else he will be loyal to the one and despise the other. You cannot serve God and mammon" Matthew 6:24 (NKJV).
15. "I Looked Into the Eyes of My Children" by Donna Reish.

Chapter 6: First Things First
1. "I do not understand my own actions. For I do not do what I want, but I do the very thing I hate" Romans 7:15 (RSV).
2. Harris, Gregg. "The Basic Home Schooling Workshop."

Noble Publishing. Audiotape, 1994.
3. Harris, Gregg. "The Advanced Home Schooling Workshop." Noble Publishing. Audiotape, 1992.

Chapter 7: Recipe for Rebellion
1. Leman, Kevin. *Making Children Mind Without Losing Yours.* New York: Dell Publishing Company, 1987.
2. "Fathers, don't aggravate your children, if you do they will become discouraged and quit trying" Colossians 3:21 (NLT).
3. Gothard, William. *How to Make an Appeal.* Oak Brook: Institute in Basic Life Principles, 1990.
4. "And you, fathers, do not provoke your children to wrath, but bring them up in the training and admonition of the Lord" Ephesians 6:4 (NKJV).
5. "A woman shall not wear anything that pertains to a man, nor shall a man put on a woman's garment, for all who do so are an abomination to the Lord your God" (Deuteronomy 22:5 NKJV).
6. "For this is the will of God, your sanctification: that you abstain from sexual immorality; that each of you know how to possess his own vessel in sanctification and honor, not in passions of lust, like the Gentiles who do not know God; that no one should take advantage of and defraud his brother in this matter..." I Thessalonians 4:3-6a (NKJV).

Chapter 8: Gotta Have Stick-tu-a-tive-ness
1. "And let us not be weary in well doing: for in due season we shall reap, if we faint not" Galatians 6:9 (KJV).
2. Kimmel, Tim. *Raising Kids for True Greatness.* Nashville: Thomas Nelson, 2006.
3. Ibid.
4. Taylor, Howard. *Spiritual Secret of Hudson Taylor.* New Kensington: Whitaker House, 1996.
5. Harris, Gregg. "The Basic Home Schooling Workshop." Noble Publishing. Audiotape, 1994.
6. Home page. *Institute in Basic Life Principles.* Online.

Accessed 31 October 2007: http://iblp.org/iblp/.

Chapter 9: I Want an Oompa Loompa Now, Daddy!

1. *Willy Wonka and the Chocolate Factory.* Dir. Mel Stuart. Perf. Gene Wilder and Peter Ostrum. Paramount Pictures. 1971.
2. "Children, obey your parents in the Lord, for this is right" Ephesians 6:1 (NKJV).
3. "Train up a child in the way he should go, And when he is old he will not depart from it" Proverbs 22:6 (NKJV).
4. "Chasten thy son while there is hope, and let not thy soul spare for his crying" Proverbs 19:18 (KJV).
5. "Then they can train the younger women to love their husbands and children" Titus 2:4 (NIV).
6. "He who spares the rod hates his son, but he who loves him is diligent to discipline him" Proverbs 13:24 (RSV).
7. "The Proverbs of Solomon: A wise son makes a glad father, But a foolish son is the grief of his mother" Proverbs 10:1 (NKJV).
8. "Chasten thy son while there is hope, and let not thy soul spare for his crying" Proverbs 19:18 (KJV).
9. "Discipline your children while there is hope. Otherwise you will ruin their lives" Proverbs 19:18 (NLT).
10. Home page. *Focus on the Family.* Online. Accessed 14 January 2008: www.family.org.
11. Home page. *Growing Families International.* Online. Accessed 14 January 2008: www.gfi.org.
12. Home page. *Solving Family Problems.* Online. Accessed 14 January 2008: www.solvefamilyproblems.com.
13. "And above all things have fervent love for one another, for 'love will cover a multitude of sins'" I Peter 4:8 (NKJV).

Chapter 10: Spank, Rattle, and Roll

1. Bradley, Reb. "Solving the Crisis in Homeschooling." 22 September 2006: www.familyministries.com/HS_Crisis.htm.
2. "Foolishness is bound up in the heart of a child; (But) the rod of correction shall drive it far from him" Proverbs

22:15 (ASV).
3. Home page. *Growing Families International.* Online. Accessed 14 January 2008: www.gfi.org.
4. Leman, Kevin. *Making Children Mind Without Losing Yours.* New York: Dell Publishing Company, 1987.
5. "He who spares the rod hates his son, but he who loves him is diligent to discipline him" Proverbs 13:24 (RSV).
6. "Chasten thy son while there is hope, and let not thy soul spare for his crying" Proverbs 19:18 (KJV).
7. "Fathers, do not aggravate your children, or they will become discouraged" Colossians 3:21 (NIV).
8. "When I was a child, I spoke as a child, I understood as a child, I thought as a child. When I became a man, I put away childish things" 1 Corinthians 13:11 (NKJV).
9. Leman, Kevin. *Making Children Mind Without Losing Yours.* New York: Dell Publishing Company, 1987.

Chapter 11: It's Not All About You

1. "In the same way, you wives, be submissive to your own husbands so that even if any of them are disobedient to the world, they may be won without a word by the behavior of their wives" I Peter 3:1 (NASB).
2. "And you shall love the LORD your God with all your heart, and with all your soul, and with all your might. And the second, like it, is this: 'You shall love your neighbor as yourself.' There is no other commandment greater than these" Mark 12:30 & 31 (NKJV).
3. "So in everything, do to others what you would have them do to you, for this sums up the Law and the Prophets" Matthew 7:12 (NIV).
4. "Where there is no vision, the people perish: but he that keepeth the law, happy is he" Proverbs 29:18 (KJV).
5. "When I was a child, I spoke as a child, I understood as a child, I thought as a child. When I became a man, I put away childish things" I Corinthians 13:11 (NKJV).
6. Strong, James. *The New Strong's Exhaustive Concordance of the Bible.* Nashville: Thomas Nelson, 1991.

7. "But you shall receive power when the Holy Spirit has come upon you; and you shall be witnesses to me in Jerusalem, and in all Judea and Samaria, and to the end of the earth" Acts 1:8 (NKJV).

Chapter 12: So How Do You Really Feel About That?

1. Lee, Harper. *To Kill a Mockingbird.* New York: Grand Central Publishing, 1988.
2. "In love of the brethren be tenderly affectioned one to another; in honor preferring one another" Romans 12:10 (ASV).
3. "Sitting down, Jesus called the Twelve and said, 'If anyone wants to be first, he must be the very last, and the servant of all'" Mark 9:35 (NIV).
4. "Moreover if your brother sins against you, go and tell him his fault between you and him alone. If he hears you, you have gained your brother" Matthew 18:15 (NKJV).
5. Home page. *Growing Families International.* Online. Accessed 14 January 2008: www.gfi.org.
6. Harris, Gregg. "The Basic Home Schooling Workshop." Noble Publishing. Audiotape, 1994.
7. Kimmel, Tim. *Raising Kids for True Greatness.* Nashville: Thomas Nelson, 2006.
8. Leman, Kevin. *Making Children Mind Without Losing Yours.* New York: Dell Publishing Company, 1987.
9. "Do not withhold good from those to whom it is due, When it is in the power of your hand to do so" Proverbs 3:27 (NKJV).
10. Home page. *Institute in Basic Life Principles.* Online. Accessed 31 October 2007: http://iblp.org/iblp/.
11. "Or when did we see You sick, or in prison, and come to You? And the kind will answer and say to them, 'Assuredly, I say to you, inasmuch as you did it to one of the least of these My brethren, you did it to Me'" Matthew 25: 39-40 (NKJV).

Chapter 13: The Socialization Trap**s**

1. Boyer, Rick. *The Socialization Trap.* Rustburg: The Learning Parent.
2. "Foolishness is bound up in the heart of a child; (But) the

rod of correction shall drive it far from him" Proverbs 22:15 (ASV).
3. "Do not be deceived: 'Bad company ruins good morals" I Corinthians 15:33 (RSV).
4. Home page. *Bold Christian Living.* Online. Accessed 16 January 2008: www.boldchristianliving.com.

Chapter 14: What a Smarty Pants!
1. Home page. *National Christian Forensics and Communications Association.* Online. Accessed 31 October 2007: www.ncfca.org.
2. "But seek first the kingdom of God and His righteousness, and all these things shall be added to you" Matthew 6:33 (NKJV).
3. Home page. *Family Man Ministries.* Online. Accessed 9 January 2008: www.familymanweb.com.
4. "But is under tutors and governors until the time appointed of the father" Galatians 4:2 (KJV).
5. Home page. *Training for Triumph Homeschool.* Online. 16 January 2008: www.tfths.com.
6. Moore, Raymond. *Better Late Than Early.* Ithaca: A.B. Publishing, 1989.
7. Moore, Raymond. *School Can Wait.* Provo: Brigham University Press, 1989.
8. "But also for this very reason, giving all diligence, add to your faith virtue, to virtue knowledge" II Peter 1:5 (NKJV).
9. Home page. *Educational Insights.* Online. Accessed 16 January 2008.

NOTES

NOTES

NOTES

NOTES

NOTES

NOTES

NOTES

NOTES

NOTES

NOTES

NOTES